TABLE OF CONTENTS

Wisdom For Crisis Times - Master Keys For Success In Times Of Change
Copyright © 1992 by *MIKE MURDOCK*
ISBN 1-56394-006-X
All publishing rights belong exclu
Published by The Wisdom Center
P. O. Box 99 • Denton, Texas 762(
1-888-WISDOM-1 (1-888-947-366
Website: www.thewisdomcenter.c

D1550600

WHY I WROTE THIS BOOK

⸻⸻►◦◄⸻⸻

God called me into the ministry at an early age. I preached my first sermon at age eight. I left Bible School in 1966 and launched into full-time evangelistic ministry to spread His Wisdom to hurting and broken people.

That was over 36 countries and 13,000 services ago. Since that time, I have shed a lot of tears...seen a lot of victories...and shared in thousands of miracles.

Every day of my life, I am convinced more and more of the awesome power God has planted within us to succeed. He has deposited the Seed of Success inside each one of us—including *you*. That Seed is Jesus.

God created you to succeed!

He gave you the gifts and talents you need to succeed in life. It is up to you to walk in the power of the Holy Spirit and in His Wisdom to discover, develop and use your gifts.

I have written this book, *Wisdom For Crisis Times*, to give you practical steps to walk through your "Seasons Of Fire."

In these times when the very foundation of the world system seems to be crumbling...and crisis is on the lips of people everywhere...this message must ring out loudly and clearly. *There Are Master Keys That Unlock The Hidden Benefits Of Any Crisis.*

In this book, I address six major areas of crisis. No matter what circumstances you face, God is your

Source of Wisdom.

Wisdom For Crisis Times will point you to the Master Keys that unlock the door to your personal happiness, peace of mind, fulfillment and success. This book will help you:

1. *Release The Champion In You.* You can overcome failure and enjoy the winning life.

2. *Understand Your Life Calling.* Discover why God created you, and accomplish the dreams hidden in your heart.

3. *Unleash Miracles Of Abundance—Finances, Health, Success And More.* You can change your circumstances, and create the tomorrow of your dreams.

4. *Recover From The Tragedy Of Divorce.* Rebuild your future, and discover the secrets to a happy marriage.

5. *Achieve Career Success And Fulfillment.* Know the right job for you. Discover your God-given talents.

6. *Learn Battle Techniques For Successful Spiritual Warfare.* Understand your enemy. Uncover his tactics. Learn how to be victorious.

Do not let satan steal the miracle God has for you today. My prayer for you is that the Wisdom of God found within the pages of this book will set you *Free* in every area of your life! That is why I wrote this book.

INTRODUCTION

———▷▷-O-◁◁———

Do you need answers...and need them *now?* Are you facing a crisis in your life that seems insurmountable...and you do not know how much longer you can take it?

Maybe your marriage has crumbled...or your family is turning against you.

Perhaps you have lost your job...or you are continually running out of money.

Maybe you are in constant physical pain or your health is failing.

Or, maybe you are not even sure why you are alive...and you have had thoughts of ending it all. Suicide.

Maybe you are facing the biggest battle you have ever had...and you do not know if you have the strength to fight any longer.

Perhaps you are not even sure what is wrong...but you know you are just not happy and fulfilled like you want to be.

You need answers.

You need *Wisdom.*

Keep reading. This is the book for you. The *Answers* to all of the above struggles is contained within these pages.

The fact that you are reading this book is proof of your *willingness* to learn.

When you are *teachable,* you are *reachable.*

So, you are *already* a Champion.

My own life has been a parade of battles and

triumphs...seasons of struggle and crisis that have produced incredible miracles. I have learned that *Struggle Is Merely Proof That You Have Not Yet Been Conquered.*

God has called and anointed me to help you achieve His dreams and goals for your life.

What is your *biggest* dream?

Yes, your obstacles might appear insurmountable today. Yes, you might be in the struggle of your lifetime right now. But get your faith up!

Your dream...inner happiness...is being kindled within your heart even as you read this page. New life and energy are about to spring forth within you. Miracles will be birthed in your spirit even as you hold this book in your hands.

So, do not give up now.

Hold on to your seat...you are about to be catapulted out of your crisis!

God is going to bless you more than you can imagine!

"Crisis Always Occurs
At The Curve Of Change."

– MIKE MURDOCK

∽ 1 ∽

WISDOM KEYS FOR TIMES OF FAILURE

Within 30 days from today, your life could be dramatically different. The crisis of failure you face today could be gone next month.

It is *your* decision.

Crisis Always Occurs At The Curve Of Change.

You see, *you* have the *power to change*...to make *new* decisions...to set in motion the lifestyle of a *Champion.* You do not have to fail in life. You *can* succeed. *It depends entirely on you.* Yes...*you!*

You do not have to be a *prisoner* of your circumstances.

You can become a *creator* of your circumstances.

Wisdom Key #1

Crisis Always Occurs At The Curve Of Change.

I am thrilled to share these powerful Wisdom Keys from the World's Greatest Book...The Holy Scriptures, "Which are able to make thee wise unto salvation through faith which is in Christ Jesus" (2 Timothy 3:15).

You can have the *heart* of a Champion.

You can have the *mind* of an Overcomer.

You can have the *spirit* of a Conqueror.

There is only One Way to inner happiness and

success. It begins with a personal relationship with Jesus Christ, and obedience to the Life Principles He taught. "We are more than conquerors through Him that loved us" (Romans 8:37).

What Is A Successful Life?

It is not necessarily a life of fame, popularity and public acceptance. Television and novels often depict the lifestyle of famous people as one of continuous pleasure...power...perfection. Tragically, the opposite is often true.

Wisdom Key #2

Success Is Satisfying Movement Toward Worthwhile Goals That God Has Scheduled For Your Life.

Fame can be burdensome, demanding and even cruel. This is easily proven by the alcoholism, drug addiction and even suicides often found among those in the limelight.

A successful life is much more than the accumulation of earthly possessions and wealth. Many biographies record the deep depression and insecurities of some of the wealthiest people in the world. Even King Solomon, in his backslidden state, cried out, "Therefore I hated life" (Ecclesiastes 2:17).

A successful life is simply a happy life.

It is a climate of enthusiasm emanating from you. You have *purpose*. You make *progress*. You know *direction*. You are *decisive*.

Success Is Satisfying Movement Toward Worthwhile Goals That God Has Scheduled For

Your Life. The Smallest Step In The Right Direction Always Creates Joy. Remember, your happiness will always begin with movement toward that which is right.

Happiness is discovering ingredients that create a successful day, then, duplicating it regularly. Any day that brings you closer to a God-given dream and goal is a successful day.

> **Wisdom Key #3**
>
> *The Smallest Step In The Right Direction Always Creates Joy.*

The Domination Factor

Let's face it. Something drives you to *dominate* the world around you...to *solve* your problems...to *master* your circumstances.

God purposefully planted this drive for mastery within you. "God said, Let us make man in Our image, after Our likeness: and let them have dominion over the fish of the sea...the fowl of the air...the cattle...all the earth, and over every creeping thing that creepeth upon the earth" (Genesis 1:26).

Note this: "Let them have dominion over the fish." God transferred the responsibility of decision-making to you and me. To dominate means to make the decision that controls another.

When you are born into the family of God, His nature is planted within you. "Whereby are given unto us exceeding great and precious promises: that by these ye might be partakers of the divine nature, having escaped the corruption that is in the world through lust" (2 Peter 1:4).

Success Is Worth The Price

▶ *A Successful Life Is Often Expensive.* It will cost you something to become a Champion. Time. Energy. Focus.

▶ *A Productive Life Is Not An Accident.* It will require some effort. Risk taking, reaching for relationships that might reject you, patient absorption of new information and ideas.

▶ *You May Even Have To Walk Away From Comfortable Circumstances And People.*

▶ *What You Are Willing To Walk Away From Determines What God Will Bring To You.*

▶ *A Successful Life Often Involves Seasons Of Pain.* Your new revelations from God may expose errors in your childhood teaching. Your early teachers may have passed on to you their distortions, prejudices and doubts. Any discovery of personal error may almost tear your very heart out.

▶ *People Never Change What They Believe Until Their Belief System Cannot Produce Something They Want.*

▶ *It Is Very Painful To Make Major Changes In Your Belief System.* This is the critical place where many people fail. They refuse to

Wisdom Key #4

What You Are Willing To Walk Away From Determines What God Will Bring To You.

acknowledge and pursue the *benefits* of change. They adapt to lack. *They forfeit their dreams to temporarily appease their fears and doubts.*

Most people fail to pursue their dreams and goals hoping to reduce their confrontations, struggles and opposition. They choose to sit as spectators in the Grandstand of Life, rather than risk the Arena of Conflict to wear the Crown of Victory.

Failure Has A Price, Too

Shockingly, most people eventually discover that it is more costly to lose than to win.

You see, failure has a price, too. What is the price of losing?

▶ *Loss Of Self-Confidence*
▶ *Inferiority*
▶ *Self-Directed Anger*
▶ *Fear Of The Future*
▶ *Low Self-Esteem That Can Even Affect Your Physical Health*
▶ *Paralysis Of Your Creative Ideas*
▶ *Depression*
▶ *Self-Destructive And Suicidal Thoughts*

Wisdom Key #5

People Never Change What They Believe Until Their Belief System Cannot Produce Something They Want.

Wisdom Key #6

Failure Is Not An Event But An Opinion.

▶ *Loss Of Favor With Friends*
▶ *And Worst Of All, You Miss God's Will And Plan For Your Life. This Is Why Success Is Worth The Price.*

4 Facts About Success

▶ *Success Is Making Progress...Movement...In The Direction Of God's Dreams And Goals For Your Life.*
▶ *Success Requires Sacrifice, Self-Discipline And Warfare.* Self must be surrendered to the will of God.
▶ *Failure Must Be Confronted And Conquered With Spiritual Weaponry.* It is normal to experience doubts regarding your efforts to live a pure, holy and victorious life for God.
▶ *You Must Take Time To Review The Benefits of Success.*

> *Wisdom Key #7*
>
> *Failure Cannot Happen In Your Life Without Your Permission.*

> *Wisdom Key #8*
>
> *Failure Will Last Only As Long As You Permit It.*

"Bless the Lord, O my soul, and forget not all His benefits: Who forgiveth all thine iniquities; Who healeth all thy diseases; Who redeemeth thy life from destruction; Who crowneth thee with lovingkindness and tender mercies; Who satisfieth thy mouth with good things; so that thy

youth is renewed like the eagle's"
(Psalm 103:2-5).

Why Is Your Success Worth Pursuing?

Note the rewards of a successful
life mentioned in these verses:
- ▶ Forgiveness
- ▶ Physical Healing For Your Body
- ▶ Protection From Your Enemies
- ▶ Promotion And Recognition
- ▶ Financial Provision
- ▶ Youthful Energy

> *Wisdom Key #9*
>
> *Any Act Of Obedience Shortens The Distance To Any Miracle You Are Pursuing.*

You Need Supernatural Power

Your personal success will never be achieved
through man-made, self-help programs that ignore
God and obedience to His Laws.

God Must Become The Center Of Your Life. "Not
that we are sufficient of ourselves to think any thing
as of ourselves; but our sufficiency is of God" (2
Corinthians 3:5). Paul said, "I can do all things
through *Christ* which strengtheneth me"
(Philippians 4:13).

The Holy Spirit And Your Success

The early disciples were weak, unstable and
powerless...*until the Holy Spirit took control of their*

lives. "But ye shall receive power, after that the Holy Ghost is come upon you" (Acts 1:8).

▶ *He Became Their Teacher.*

▶ *He Revealed The Nature Of God And His Purposes.*

▶ *He Imparted His Power For Them To Heal The Sick, Raise The Dead And Cast Out Evil Spirits* (see Matthew 10:8). "And these signs shall follow them that believe; In My name shall they cast out devils; they shall speak with new tongues; they shall take up serpents; and if they drink any deadly thing, it shall not hurt them; they shall lay hands on the sick, and they shall recover" (Mark 16:17,18).

It was the Holy Spirit and His revelations that turned these early disciples from weaklings into Champions.

Your 4 Steps Into A Successful Life

Four outstanding ingredients are easily seen in these lives touched by God. Truly, the early disciples enjoyed a successful life.

▶ *They Had An Accurate Picture Of God And His Nature.*

▶ *They Recognized The Limited Capabilities Of Their Enemy, Satan.*

▶ *They Focused Their Ministry On Healing Hurting People And Solving Their Problems.*

▶ *They Respected Themselves As Chosen Vessels Of Healing.*

Now, let's apply their secrets to your own life today.

1.   *Reconstruct A More Accurate Picture Of God.* He is not a harsh dictator wanting to smash earthlings at the slightest sign of error. Rather, He is a God of Miracles...Love...Compassion...and Healing. "Yea, I have loved thee with an everlasting love...with lovingkindness have I drawn thee" (Jeremiah 31:3). God is "not willing that any should perish, but that all should come to repentance" (2 Peter 3:9).

> ▶ *He Is Your Companion.* "For He hath said, I will never leave thee, nor forsake thee" (Hebrews 13:5).
> ▶ *He Is Your Father.* "For ye have not received the spirit of bondage again to fear; but ye have received the Spirit of adoption, whereby we cry, Abba, Father" (Romans 8:15).
> ▶ *He Is Your Protector.* "What time I am afraid, I will trust in Thee" (Psalm 56:3).
> ▶ *He Is Your Healer.* "I am the Lord that healeth thee" (Exodus 15:26).
> ▶ *He Is Your Provider.* "But my God shall supply all your need according to His riches in glory by Christ Jesus" (Philippians 4:19).
> ▶ *He Is Your Teacher.* "I will instruct thee and teach thee in the way which thou shalt go: I will guide thee with Mine eye" (Psalm 32:8).
> ▶ *He Is Your Giver Of Gifts.* "Every good gift and every perfect gift is from above, and cometh down from the Father of lights, with Whom is no variableness, neither

shadow of turning" (James 1:17).

Will He *Always* Love You? Will He *Always* Forgive You? Will He *Always* Heal You? Will He *Always* Restore You?

Absolutely. Yes! "For I am the Lord, I change not" (Malachi 3:6). "Jesus Christ the same yesterday, and today, and for ever" (Hebrews 13:8).

> **Wisdom Key #10**
>
> *God Always Rewards Reachers.*

Will He Show Favor, Mercy And Forgiveness To You Personally? Yes! "God is no respecter of persons" (Acts 10:34). "Him that cometh to me I will in no wise cast out" (John 6:37).

Call on God. Respect His invitation to a relationship.

It has been said that your opinion of your earthly father often influences your opinion of your Heavenly Father. So if your parents were not loving and caring, you might need an extra touch from God to get a more accurate understanding of the depth of His love and interest in your life and happiness.

> **Wisdom Key #11**
>
> *Faith Is Confidence In The Integrity Of God.*

This explains most of our difficulty with our faith. If you misunderstand and misinterpret God, it may be difficult for you to believe His Word.

Faith is simply confidence in His integrity.

2.   *Recognize The Limited Capabilities Of Your Enemy, Satan.* "Submit yourselves therefore to God. Resist the devil, and he will flee from you" (James 4:7).

Satan fears you and the authority that you have

over him through Christ. You are a joint-heir with Christ. Therefore, all things have been placed under your feet or control...including satan! "And hath put all things under *his* feet" (Ephesians 1:22).

3 Things Satan Cannot Do

1. *He Cannot Stop God From Loving You.*
2. *He Cannot Stop God From Hearing You.*
3. *He Cannot Stop God From Responding To You.*

Command satan to take his hands off your life...to stop harassing your children who have been dedicated to the Lord...*to get off your property and out of your life!* "Greater is He that is in you, than he that is in the world" (1 John 4:4).

3. *Reach Out To Someone Close To You Who Is Hurting.* This is the Miracle Key in defeating depression, loneliness and emptiness in your life.

> ▶ A successful company studies how to meet the *needs of its customers.*
> ▶ Successful parents focus on the *needs of their children.*
> ▶ An employee who gets promoted is the one

Wisdom Key #12

Satan Cannot Linger Where He Is Firmly Resisted.

Wisdom Key #13

What You Make Happen For Others, God Will Make Happen For You.

who studies the *needs of his boss.* "Let no
man seek his own, but every man
another's wealth" (1 Corinthians 10:24).

*Your Contribution To Others Is The Same
Measuring Cup God Uses To Make Contributions To
Your Own Life.* So it is with a successful, winning,
happy life. "Look not every man on his own things,
but every man also on the things of others"
(Philippians 2:4). "Knowing that whatsoever good
thing any man doeth, the same shall he receive of
the Lord" (Ephesians 6:8).

Find a damaged heart.

Discern a confused mind.

Feel a broken life close to you.

Pour the healing oil of Jesus on those wounds.
*It will open Heaven's Windows of Blessing on your
own life.*

This is *The Greatest Law On Earth*, The Law
Of Seed-Faith. It is *Sowing What You Have
Received From God Into Someone Else In Need.*

Remember...

▶ *Your Seed Is Anything You Possess That
Can Help Someone Else Achieve Their
Dreams And Goals.*

▶ *Your Harvest Is Whatever God Can Do
That Helps You Achieve Your Dreams And
Goals.*

When you open your hand to help others, God
opens His hand to reward you. (I have written much
more on Seed-faith in a later chapter.)

4. *Respect Yourself As A Chosen Vessel Of Healing.* The Israelites who left Egypt under Moses *never* entered Canaan, the land of abundance. You see, they had been peasants and slaves under Egyptian bondage. And they could never shake that *slaveship mentality* even though they had left Egypt!

They *thought* like slaves.

They *talked* like slaves.

They *behaved* like slaves.

They fretted. They fumed. They doubted their capability to overcome giants in the Great Land of Promise, Canaan. They even labeled and named themselves as *"Grasshoppers"* when they saw the giants!*

Wisdom Key #14

Your Words Are The Vehicles To Your Future.

Joshua and Caleb were different.

They respected their Creator.

They respected *themselves.*

They saw themselves as victors, overcomers, and conquerors. "Let us go up at once, and possess it; for we are *well able to overcome it"* (Numbers 13:30).

They were not complainers.

They were not murmurers.

They were not doubters.

They possessed "another spirit" (Numbers 14:24).

Winners never magnify their personal weaknesses. They *know* their God will use any flaw

---

*Recommended Tapes: Grasshopper Complex (six cassettes). Write: Mike Murdock • P. O. Box 99 • Denton, TX 76202.

to reveal His power and grace.

"My grace is sufficient for thee: for My strength is made perfect in weakness" (2 Corinthians 12:9).

> ▶ *Respect The New Nature God Has Given You As His Special Child.* "If any man be in Christ, he is a new creature: old things are passed away...all things are...new" (2 Corinthians 5:17).

Wisdom Key #15

Crisis Is Merely Concentrated Information.

> ▶ *Cherish God's Authority And Association With You.* Doing this unleashes His Power and Might over your enemy, satan. "Through God we shall do valiantly: for He it is that shall tread down our enemies" (Psalm 108:13).

God has already given you the power to succeed in life. You are already a Champion. Yes, you will go through this crisis...but it is up to you to use this time of crisis as a stepping stone to success.

Go for it!

☙ 2 ☙

WISDOM KEYS FOR CRISIS IN YOUR LIFE PURPOSE

You were created for a *purpose*.

There is a perfect plan for your life. No matter what crisis you face today, never forget God created you for a specific purpose...a specific Assignment.

▶ He *Loves* You.

▶ He *Planned* You.

▶ He *Scheduled* Your Birth.

▶ He Is *Forever Linked* To You.

In fact, God loves you so much that He sent His Son, Jesus, to help you through this time of crisis.

Jesus is a friend who will never leave you. He will stick with you closer than a blood brother. "For He hath said, I will never leave thee, nor forsake thee" (Hebrews 13:5).

Jesus wants to help you fulfill all the dreams God created you to accomplish on this earth. All you have to do is *ask* Him. "Ask, and ye shall receive, that your joy may be full" (John 16:24).

Wisdom
Key #16

*Your
Purpose Is
Not Your
Decision
But Your
Discovery.*

Trust The Wisdom Of Your Creator

When I was a teenager, I heard

a story about a farmer whose son went off to college. The father was a bit concerned over the exposure his son would have to atheistic teaching. He knew how articulate and seductive these skilled communicators could be in spreading their own *disease of doubt.*

Frustration is always contagious.

The fears of the father were eventually confirmed. His son returned home for a visit, obviously grappling with his faith in God.

As they were conversing one day under an old oak tree, the son suddenly blurted out, "Dad, I just can't believe in God anymore. Why, look at those pumpkins over there on the ground. They are big and heavy, yet have small and tender vines.

"But this big oak tree, capable of supporting the weight of the pumpkins, only produces tiny acorns. If there was really an intelligent God of this universe, He would have placed the pumpkin on this oak tree and the tiny acorn on the fragile vine."

Suddenly, an acorn fell from the tree, bouncing lightly off the top of the young man's head.

As the truth slowly dawned, he sheepishly spoke, "Dad, thank God that was not a pumpkin!"

Throughout your lifetime, you too, may question the existence of your Creator.

Your *logic* will always compete with your *faith.*

Your *mind* will compete with your *heart.*

A book is proof of an *author.*

A poem is proof of a *poet.*

A song is proof of a *composer.*

A product is proof of a *manufacturer.*

Creation is proof of a *Creator.*

Only Fools Think They Arrived First. "The fool

hath said in his heart, There is no God" (Psalm 14:1).

God exists.

The world is arranged... therefore, an *Arranger must exist.*

So let's not toil over the *focus of fools*—"Does God exist?" Rather:

▶ Why Did He Make *You?*
▶ What Is His Purpose In *Your* Life?
▶ What Does He Want *You* To *Do*?
▶ What Does He Want *You* To *Know*?
▶ What Does He Want *You* To *Be*?

> *Wisdom Key #17*
>
> *The Proof Of God's Presence Far Outweighs The Proof Of His Absence.*

You see, someday it will hit you like a bolt of lightning—your Creator is a *Planner*...incredibly *organized*...meticulous with details...and like any successful manufacturer, He is totally committed to the success of His product...*You.*

Why Did God Create You?

1.   *You Were Created To Be An Instrument Of Pleasure To God* (see Revelation 4:11).

You *affect* God.

You have the power to *pleasure* Him.

You have the power to *displeasure* Him.

The Bible teaches us how to have a *relationship* with Him. "Thou hast created all things, and for Thy pleasure they are and were created" (Revelation 4:11). The Bible is His personal profile, His personal likes and dislikes, His dreams and expectations.

▶ *He Is Touched With The Feelings Of Our*

Infirmities and "was in all points tempted like...we are, yet without sin" (Hebrews 4:15).

▶ *He Loves People.* "For God so loved the world, that He gave His only begotten Son, that whosoever believeth in Him should not perish, but have everlasting life" (John 3:16).

▶ *He Craves To Be Understood.* "Let him that glorieth glory in this, that he understandeth and knoweth Me, that I am the Lord which exercise lovingkindness, judgment, and righteousness...for in these things I delight, saith the Lord" (Jeremiah 9:24).

▶ *Prayer Pleasures Him.* "If My people...shall humble themselves, and pray, and seek My face, and turn from their wicked ways; then will I...forgive their sin, and will heal their land" (2 Chronicles 7:14).

▶ *Healing Pleasures Him.*

"How God anointed Jesus of Nazareth with the Holy Ghost and with power: Who went about doing good, and healing all that were oppressed of the devil; for God was with Him" (Acts 10:38). "Who forgiveth all thine iniquities; Who healeth all thy diseases" (Psalm 103:3).

"Who His own self bare our sins in His own body on the tree...by whose stripes ye were healed" (1 Peter 2:24).

▶ *Evangelization Pleasures Him.* "And He said unto

Wisdom Key #18

Prayer Is One Of The Proofs That You Truly Respect God.

them, Go ye into all the world, and preach the gospel to every creature" (Mark 16:15).

▶ *Praise Pleasures Him.* "Enter into His gates with thanksgiving, and into His courts with praise: be thankful unto Him, and bless His name" (Psalm 100:4).

"Oh that men would praise the Lord for His goodness, and for His wonderful works to the children of men!" (Psalm 107:15).

2. *When You Pleasure God, He Pleasures You.*

"If thou shalt hearken diligently unto the voice of the Lord thy God, to observe and to do all His commandments...the Lord thy God will set thee on high above all nations...And all these blessings shall come on thee, and overtake thee, if thou shalt hearken unto the voice of the Lord thy God" (Deuteronomy 28:1,2).

> *Wisdom Key #19*
>
> *God Never Forgets Anyone Who Makes Him Feel Good.*

▶*Picture A Reward System.*

Think of an invisible cord linking your heart to the heart of God. Whatever emotion you create in His heart is the *same feeling* you create in your own heart—good or bad. Joy or frustration.

This means that when you disappoint Him, you will feel it too...through *personal* frustration, guilt and emptiness.

Likewise, when you pleasure Him, you will create (within yourself) an almost unexplainable, exhilarating joy and enthusiasm. "If ye be willing and obedient, ye shall eat the good of the land" (Isaiah 1:19).

3. *God Is Pleasured Through Daily Acts Of Obedience That Progressively Complete His Dreams And Goals In Your Life.*

There is a *reason* for His commands and instructions. It is *not* to create a *King-Peasant* relationship. Each task He requests is a *piece* of tomorrow's Puzzle of Success. His restrictions and insistence on holy living simply *eliminate distraction* ...and help you *concentrate on your dream.*

Obedience is cooperating with God to achieve your goals. It may even create a season of pain *at first.* But it is the *Golden Link in the Chain of Success.* "And whatsoever we ask, we receive of Him, because we keep His commandments, and do those things that are pleasing in His sight" (1 John 3:22).

> **Wisdom Key #20**
>
> *Obedience Is The Only Thing God Has Ever Required Of Man.*

4. *Your Strongest Desires, Talents And Opportunities Reveal God's Calling And Dream For Your Life.* What do you *enjoy* doing? What would you *attempt* to do if you knew it were *impossible to fail?*

You *already* possess *special gifts and talents* from the Lord: "Having then gifts differing according to the grace that is given to us, whether prophecy...Or ministry...or he that teacheth...Or he that exhorteth... he that giveth...he that ruleth...he that sheweth mercy" (Romans 12:6-8).

God wants you to *pursue* those dreams and goals that you *love.* What you desire the most is usually *what you are already gifted to accomplish.*

You are *not* an accident.

You *are* a divine creation, designed for something specific. "Before I formed thee in the belly, I knew thee; and before thou camest forth out of the womb I sanctified thee, and I ordained thee a prophet unto the nations" (Jeremiah 1:5).

He revealed His calling to Jeremiah—and He will do the same for you!

5. *Successful People Find Daily Significance In 24 Hours Of Progress.*

Success is *movement*...progress... toward a God-inspired goal. You were created to *produce*. Multiply. Replenish. Rule. Increase.

The *pastor* strives to increase the membership.

The *evangelist* struggles to get more souls saved.

The *husband* works hard to buy a large home for his family.

A *productive* person is usually a *happy* person, fulfilled and self-confident. Depression is often created by *idleness*. "Whatsoever thy hand findeth to do, do it with thy might" (Ecclesiastes 9:10). "By much slothfulness the building decayeth; and through idleness of the hands the house droppeth through" (Ecclesiastes 10:18).

6. *Your Seeds Of Faith Determine Your Season Of Increase.* "But this I say, He which soweth sparingly shall reap...sparingly; and

> **Wisdom Key #21**
>
> *What You Love Is A Clue To Your Assignment And Purpose In Life.*

> **Wisdom Key #22**
>
> *People Who Feel Great About Themselves Produce Great Results.*

he which soweth bountifully shall reap...bountifully"
(2 Corinthians 9:6).

You have received something from God—*something you can give away*—called a *Seed*.

Whatever God has in His hand is a Harvest.

Sow *diligence* into your job. Sow *time* and *love* into your family. Sow *finances* into His work.

There are many "parts" of you— your time...energy...talent...friendships...money. *Each part is a Seed.* When you sow it, wrapped with your faith in God for a *Harvest*, you create a guaranteed Season of Blessing and Increase in your life.

> **Wisdom Key #23**
>
> **He Multiplies Your Seed Back Into Your Life Where You Need It The Most.**

These continuous harvests create waves of joy, fulfillment and happiness throughout your entire lifetime.

Study the above six guidelines regularly. These are principles of Wisdom from the Bible—the Word of God. Each one is an important link in your discovery of your *purpose* in life.

Your *happiness is the product of that discovery.* "If thou draw out thy soul to the hungry...then shall thy light rise in obscurity, and thy darkness be as the noon day...thou shalt be like a watered garden, and like a spring of water, whose waters

> **Wisdom Key #24**
>
> **Your Seed Is Anything God Has Given You To Sow Into Someone Else.**

fail not" (Isaiah 58:10,11).

Reach out to help someone else today. When you do, God will see to it that your dark time of crisis will subside...and the light of happiness will flood your heart like a sunrise.

Something Very Wonderful Is Close To You Today.

Wisdom Key #25

Your Reaction To Someone In Trouble Determines God's Reaction To You The Next Time You Are In Trouble.

*"Intolerance Of Your Present
Creates Your Future."*

– MIKE MURDOCK

⇝ 3 ⇜

WISDOM KEYS FOR SURVIVING FINANCIAL CRISIS

⟿⟾

What is the biggest need in your life right now?
What desired *miracle* is on your mind the most?
What *dream* dominates your heart?
Are you facing a *financial* crisis this very moment?
Do you lay awake at night tormented by unpaid bills piled high?
Do you sometimes feel overwhelmed by the waves of futility?
The stress of financial crisis can be too much at times...past-due bills...phone calls from creditors...repossession...eviction notices...demand letters...collection lawsuits...*bankruptcy.*
I know what financial crisis feels like.
I know the feeling of losing everything you have.
You see, I have been there. *I know what it means to pace the floor with tears streaming down my face...tormented, angry—yes—even humiliated...staggered by problems that seemed insurmountable.*
I visualized life like a bank vault containing valuable treasures. My heart pounded with frustrated anticipation of the hidden treasures *my*

spirit knew existed inside.

But I just could not seem to find the key that would unlock it.

It was even more frustrating to hear others testify of "miracles" in their lives. I ached to discover *the hidden mystery behind it all.*

What Was Their Secret??

It is called Seed-faith. Since I learned the incredible power of Seed-faith, *my life has never been the same.*

That is why I am thrilled to share the Principle of Seed-faith with you today through this book.

What I Taught My Son

Not too many years ago, my son Jason learned the miracle of Seed-faith.

One day he broke down weeping. He was very worried over some of his grades in school. His voice broke, "Dad, math is hard for me. I'm just not doing well in math. I just can't seem to catch on."

Patiently, I listened for a few moments, and then related my own experience with algebra.

Wisdom Key #26

Intolerance Of The Present Creates A Future.

"Baby, I had the same problem when I was in school. In fact, I failed my first six weeks of algebra!"

I continued to share with him a similar dilemma in my own school days. I just could not grasp why we were using *letters* instead of *numbers!* I knew I had to *do something* about it, but was too embarrassed and ashamed to talk about my problem to anyone.

Finally, I became desperate.

As long as you can endure a problem, you will not reach for a remedy.

When I began to think about my next report-card day, I became motivated to find a solution.

My teacher suggested that I come in after school for two hours until I could catch on. Two hours— as if 7½ hours were not enough already!! I was *horrified.* Especially when I thought about all my friends playing and having fun while I studied. But I knew I had to do it.

> *Wisdom Key #27*
>
> *Whatever God Has Already Given To You Will Create Anything Else He Has Promised You.*

The passing grade would be worth my sacrificing those golden hours of fun.

Good Things Take Extra Effort

I then explained to Jason how the good things of life sometimes take a little longer to obtain. A little more sacrifice is required.

I talked about friendships being built stronger through *hours* spent together; how experts become knowledgeable when they devote their *time* and total attention to discovering the secrets of the special topic they are studying.

I reminded him that greatness costs...but the rewards are well worth the price. I encouraged him to invest extra time in private talks with his teacher... to give total focus and attention each evening to his math.

Those hours were like Seeds—producing knowledge, high marks and lifetime benefits.

You Always Have Enough To Create More

You see, I was really explaining the Principle of Seed-faith to Jason. He could *create* the grades he wanted...by *sowing* his *Time.*

What you have is a *Seed.*

What God has is a *Harvest.*

You sow your Seed...in faith...that God will honor it by returning to you the desired harvest.

You Are Creating Tomorrow Right Now

Your tomorrow can be anything you want it to be...a tomorrow filled with happiness...good health... spiritual power...financial freedom... a vibrant marriage...*Anything.*

That is what Seed-faith is all about: creating a beautiful future by *trusting God enough to sow* your Seeds of love, time, and finances back into His world for a desired harvest.

When you sow bad Seeds, you stain the future with heartache. When you sow good Seeds, you unleash the potential of thousands of miracles (see Galatians 6:8).

Wisdom Key #28

When You Let Go Of What Is In Your Hand, God Will Let Go Of What Is In His Hand.

5 Powerful Points On Seed-Faith

1.   *God Is Your Total Source For Every Good*

Thing You Want To Happen In Your Life. "Every good...and...perfect gift is from above, and cometh down from the Father of lights, with Whom is no variableness" (James 1:17).

Your loved ones may often become His *channels*...but *He is your true Source.*

Your boss and company officials may be favorable and generous to you...but, *God is your Source.* This is so important. If you do not understand this, you will become resentful of any person you believe to be slowing your progress or "robbing" you of success. "For promotion cometh neither from the east, nor from the west, nor from the south, But God is the judge: He putteth down one, and setteth up another" (Psalm 75:6,7).

2.   *You Don't Have A Thing God Didn't Give You Anyway.* Your talents...energy...friendships...finances...ideas...blessings of every kind...are gifts from God (see 1 Corinthians 4:7).

3.   *Your Seed Is Anything You Have That Could Benefit And Advantage Someone Else.* An act of kindness...your prayer for a sick loved one...a thoughtful word of encouragement...your tithes and offerings to the work of God... *Anything* you *do* or *say* that could help someone is a *Seed.*

You are a Seed.

4.   *We Are Commanded To Sow Good Seed Into The Lives Of*

Wisdom Key #29

Your Seed May Leave Your Hand, But It Will Never Leave Your Life. It Goes Into Your Future Where It Multiplies.

Others. "Withhold not good from them to whom it is due, when it is in the power of thine hand to do it" (Proverbs 3:27). "As we have therefore opportunity, let us do good unto all men, especially unto them who are of the household of faith" (Galatians 6:10).

> *Wisdom Key #30*
>
> *Your Seed Is The Only Influence You Have Over Your Future.*

Somebody needs you today. Perhaps you know a bit of information that is vital to their success. Will you share it? That is your Seed into their life.

When a ministry asks you for financial assistance on a project, *your response is your Seed.*

Does your boss need you to go the "extra mile?" *Plant it as a Seed unto the Lord.* "Servants, be obedient to them that are your masters according to the flesh...With good will doing service, as to the Lord, and not to men: Knowing that whatsoever good thing any man doeth, the same shall he receive of the Lord" (Ephesians 6:5,7,8).

Attentiveness to the unique needs of your mate can produce miraculous results. That is sowing good Seed!

5.   *Seed-Faith Is Giving Something To God In Expectation That He Will Multiply It Back Where You Need It The Most.*

Elijah taught this to the starving widow and her son in 1 Kings 17. He asked her to sow a *portion* of her last meal and expect God's supernatural supply *as a result of her sowing.*

Sacrifice was not mentioned. His own needs were not the subject of discussion.

Her personal harvest was the only reason Elijah gave her to sow. "And she went and did according to the saying of Elijah: and she, and he, and her house, did eat many days. And the barrel of meal wasted not, neither did the cruse of oil fail, according to the word of the Lord, which He spake by Elijah" (1 Kings 17:15,16).

> **Wisdom Key #31**
>
> *Your Seed Is A Monument Of Trust In The Mind Of God.*

This exciting principle will work for the needs in your life.

> ▶ *Your Seed Is What Produces A Harvest.*
> ▶ *Your Faith Is What Brings It To You.*
> ▶ *Your Seed Is What God Multiplies.*
> ▶ *Your Faith Is Why God Multiplies It.*

Tomorrow Is Not Here Yet

Picture this tragic scenario in the tiny cottage in the village of Zarephath. The obituary has been prepared. The widow slowly prepares her last meal for her son and herself.

Tomorrow seems hopeless.

Futility is etched in every wrinkle on her face. *But God Saw Her.*

Let me say something to you, my dear friend. *God Sees You, Too.* He knows where you hurt the most. He knows *who* has stripped you of your joy, your victory, your possessions.

And He is not through blessing you today. So, Tomorrow Is Not Here Yet...You Can Make It Anything You Want It To Be.

Elijah was a Seed-faith Prophet. He saw more

than her Seed. *He saw the future her Seed could produce.* He talked to her about her *receiving*...A Divine Supernatural Harvest.

She did not argue that she "deserved to die."

She did not quarrel over the *theology* of it.

She did not whine that it sounded "selfish and greedy."

She simply obeyed.

She wanted to *Live.* I am sure that she despised poverty and hated her circumstances of lack.

She knew that she had to change her belief system before she could change what was happening in her life.

She had 4 characteristics common among Champions:

> ▶ *The Ability* To Recognize A Man Of God When She Saw Him.
> ▶ *The Willingness* To Listen To The Wisdom Of His Instructions.
> ▶ *The Faith* To Sow A Seed Of Faith Into Her Future.
> ▶ *The Recognition* That Her Future Was In Her Seed.

She discovered that she already had enough to *Create* what she did *not* have.

You too, can write a new page in your life. You can create any

Wisdom Key #32

What You Believe Is Creating Your Present Circumstances.

Wisdom Key #33

Whatever You Have In Your Hand Is What God Will Use To Create Your Future.

tomorrow you need.

Seed-faith is the most powerful Law of Increase I have ever discovered. You too, can use it to unlock the door to the miracles you need in your life today.

Expect Good Things To Start Happening To You!

Begin to look for new ways to put the Law of Seed-faith to work in your life, your family, your job, and the work of God.

Start *expecting* extraordinary blessings to happen for you.

Your harvest is *closer than you may realize.*

I wrote a song several years ago:

> *Wisdom Key #34*
>
> *When Your Seed Leaves Your Hand, Your Harvest Will Leave The Warehouse Of Heaven Toward You!*

I Started Living (When I Started Giving To God)[1]

There are pages of life
I truly regret
Lost everything I had
Stayed deep in debt.
Then one day I happened to read
In Malachi chapter three
That my release would bring an increase for me.
I started living when I started giving to God.
I started living when I started giving to God.

[1]Used by permission. Win-Song Productions, Inc. Mike Murdock

Pressed down, shaken together,
Running over, He's blessing me.
I started living when I started giving to God.
Pressed down, shaken together,
Running over, He's blessing me.
I started living when I started giving to God.

My dear partner, something good is being scheduled for your life!! Sow your way out of financial crisis and into a divine harvest. You *Can* create your tomorrow...*Today*...through Seed-faith.

❧ 4 ❧

WISDOM KEYS DURING THE CRISIS OF DIVORCE

Divorce is a *wrenching* time.

It is the tearing apart of two souls whose union has been honored by God as a marriage.

The scars run deep.

The heartache is *indescribable.*

The *memories* are forever burned into the tormented minds of those who suffer it.

Unfortunately, millions of people endure the crisis of divorce, but never *extract the education* it offers.

The stigma always leaves a stain.

Even well-meaning ministers mistakenly label the divorced with those who commit rape, murder, theft or even abortion. The fact that many are *victims* of divorce has never even occurred to them. But divorce is real. And it is happening far too often.

Theologians can argue.

Ministers may debate.

I simply want to help you draw from the well of wisdom during this time of crisis.

My Own Experience

I was left emotionally devastated following the

breakup of my thirteen years of marriage. I could not believe it had really happened to *me*.

I felt I had no one to turn to for comfort, understanding or direction. My closest friends could only shake their heads, shrug their shoulders and mumble a few words, "It will be all right in due time."

The loneliness was torturous.

That is why I am including this chapter. I know that you, too, may be carrying a Volcano of Pain within you.

Your mind may be in shreds.

You may even want to die.

Humiliation. Fear. Confusion. Rejection. Pain. Worst of all, help-lessness. *Total helplessness.* And the few who seem to care rarely know what to do to help you.

I have been there.

Your mind continues to replay *again and again* the memories of your past.

Like a visible growth on your face, divorce is like a scar that never seems to go away. You just cannot seem to shake it. You feel that everyone is talking about you, looking at you and questioning your integrity.

Probably nothing more painful will happen in your life than divorce. It may seem like the longest midnight of your lifetime.

Wisdom Key #35

Your Struggle Is Proof You Have Not Yet Been Conquered.

6 Serious And Personal Questions

You must honestly answer these six questions

before you can create a new future.

1.	*Do You Truly Want To Recover?* Your recovery may be progressive, not necessarily instantaneous.

2.	*Do You Want To Be Totally Healed?* Time does not heal you. *God* heals you. If time heals, God is unnecessary.

3.	*Do You Believe God Can Restore You Into Complete Fellowship So You Can Learn To Trust And Lean On Him Again For Your Future?*

4.	*Are You Willing To Be Delivered From The Bitterness, Resentment And Hostility That Might Still Linger Within The Crevices Of Your Heart?*

5.	*Are You Willing To Forgive And Release Your Former Mate To God For His Judgment, Correction And Accountability?*

6.	*Are You Willing To Invest Time And Effort In Rebuilding Your Life?*

I believe you are. Or you would not be reading this book right now. You are reaching. Seeking. Listening.

God respects you for doing so.

Why Marriage Anyway?

My close friend, Pastor Randy Morrison, often says, "If you don't understand the *purpose* of something, you will abuse it." Millions do not really grasp the purpose of marriage.

Following my divorce, I experienced great bitterness. Resentment. I hated being alone, but I also despised having a need for someone in my life. I wanted to be *totally independent.* I did not want to need someone else.

I even questioned the benefits of marriage. In fact, I worked hard to sell myself on "being single." I was determined that:

I would *never* be hurt again.

I would *never* trust again.

I would *never* empty my life into another.

I would *never* reveal my weaknesses to another.

I would *never* lean on or permit the necessity of someone in my life again.

I viewed those who appeared happily married as actually ignorant of the upcoming tragedy that would soon appear in their lives.

Yet, I had to admit that:

▶ *Marriage Was God's Idea.* Not satan's. Not even Adam's.

▶ *God Intended Marriage To Be A Benefit, An Asset To Mankind.* "God said, It is not good that the man should be alone; I will make...an help meet for him" (Genesis 2:18). So God joined Adam with Eve and the human race began.

▶ *Marriage Is Two People Becoming One In Spirit, Vision And Purpose.* "God made them male and female. For this cause shall a man leave his father and mother, and cleave to his wife; And they twain shall be one flesh...What therefore God hath joined together, let not man put asunder" (Mark 10:6-9).

▶ *Marriage Is To Be An Exchange Of Blessing And Favor.* "Whoso findeth a wife findeth a good thing, and obtaineth favor of the

Lord" (Proverbs 18:22).

▶ *Marriage Is Compared To The Union Of Jesus Christ And The Church.* "For the husband is the head of the wife, even as Christ is the head of the church: and He is the Saviour of the body. Husbands, love your wives, even as Christ also loved the church, and gave Himself for it" (Ephesians 5:23,25).

Your Marriage Has One Enemy, Who Uses Many Weapons

Whether you are married or divorced, you need to be reminded that your marriage was fought from the very beginning.

Your only real enemy in marriage is satan. His attack on your home and marriage is ultimately an attack on God, Jesus and the Church.

You probably entered your marriage with joy, anticipating a lifetime of happiness together. Suddenly, unexpected things happened. Personalities collide.

Whether you realized it or not, your relationship was attacked from unseen, outside satanic forces. "Be sober, be vigilant; because your adversary the devil, as a roaring lion, walketh about, seeking whom he may devour" (1 Peter 5:8).

One of the greatest fears you may experience following divorce is *remarriage* and the possibility of a *repeated failure*. The thought can be devastating. That is why some people who re-marry experience divorce again. Few discover the *true* enemy that unraveled their first marriage.

Take a moment to review some possible problems and their source.

Possible Entry Points Or Weapons Often Used To Attack Marriages

The devil is a thief, a robber. "The thief cometh not, but for to steal, and to kill and to destroy" (John 10:10).

His attacks are not simply to destroy your marriage, but to sever your relationship with God. His goal is to *discredit the integrity of God* in your mind.

Satan constantly searches for *Weapons, or Entry Points*—a friendship, sickness, finances.

That is why it is important for you to review the pieces of the puzzle to *discern and define the tragic thread that unravels the fabric of your life.*

> *Wisdom Key #36*
>
> *Satan Is The Source Of All The Pain You Will Experience During Your Lifetime.*

Here Are 6 Entry Points Satan Often Uses

1. *Weapon Of Unwise Friendships.* Friendships unravel and destroy, or build and reinforce your vision and dream.

Which friends help reinforce your marriage with the presence of God and subconsciously motivate you to love your mate more than ever? They are probably *beneficial* to your marriage.

But if the fragmented and frazzled marriages of your friends contain constant bickering and arguing, believe me, *this will affect your own marriage* when these friends are in your presence. "He that walketh with wise men shall be wise: but a companion of fools shall be destroyed" (Proverbs 13:20). "Be not deceived: evil communications corrupt good manners" (1 Corinthians 15:33).

2. *Weapon Of Sickness.* When your mate is sick, the love relationship will be affected. That is one of the reasons I believe sickness and disease are satanic.

Sickness is a Thief of Love.

Thief Of Love[2]

It stole into my home in the midnight hour.
I discerned not its goal, its strength,
Nor its power.
Little by little, the marriage declined.
Sickness stole the love once so divine.

Sickness steals time and affection. While medicine is a tool ordained of God to accelerate physical healing, you must be sensitive to the fact that medication, "uppers and downers," can eventually *alter the personality* of someone you love. It can actually destroy your relationship.

Sickness is often a "third party" that pollutes, stains and destroys a successful marriage. It has

[2]Poem by Mike Murdock. Copyright Wisdom International, Inc.

hurt more marriages than anyone will ever realize or admit.

3.   *Weapon Of The Unbridled Tongue.* This is one of the most dangerous, and one you must *learn* to overcome. One unkind statement can poison twenty years of relationship.

That is the importance of having the Holy Spirit in your life. He can keep the fragrance of compassion in every word uttered in your home. "Death and life are in the power of the tongue...they that love it shall eat the fruit thereof" (Proverbs 18:21).

I wrote a song several years ago:

The Kindest Word (Is An Unkind Word Unsaid)[3]

The kindest word is an unkind word unsaid.
The kindest letter is an unkind letter unread.
Words unspoken leave hearts unbroken.
The kindest word is an unkind word unsaid.

"The tongue...boasteth great things. Behold, how great a matter a little fire kindleth! And the tongue is...a world of iniquity...it defileth the whole body, and setteth on fire the course of nature; and it is set on fire of hell...But the tongue can no man tame; it is an unruly evil, full of deadly poison" (James 3:5-8).

4.   *Weapon Of Unrealistic Expectations.* We often want our mates to be the *total* source of our joy and satisfaction in life. Subconsciously, we attempt to make them our "gods."

[3]Used by permission. Win-Song Productions, Inc. Mike Murdock

But God will never allow a husband or a wife to be a *substitute* for Him. In fact, He encourages us to find satisfaction through our own relationship with Him, independent of what others may do. "Let every man prove his own work, and then shall he have rejoicing in himself alone, and not in another" (Galatians 6:4).

5. *Weapon Of Financial Problems.* It has been said that financial problems are the number one cause for divorce. When there are money problems in marriage, mates begin to blame each other.

Overspending, pride of ownership and covetousness can only be cured through faithful stewardship. Victory comes through total focus on God and the willingness to be *patient* after sowing Seeds of diligence and finances into God's world. "So the eyes of man are never satisfied" (Proverbs 27:20). "But my God shall supply all your need according to His riches in glory by Christ Jesus" (Philippians 4:19).

6. *Weapon Of Spiritual Isolation.* It is vital that your marriage be under the covering of a man of God in your *community*. Submission to an effective and knowledgeable *pastor* and a thriving *church home is a protection against this deadly weapon.* "Not forsaking the assembling of ourselves together...but exhorting one another" (Hebrews 10:25).

It is important that the *husband* be the *priest of the home,* presenting spiritual leadership to his mate and family on a *daily* basis. When this is lacking, the foundation for a good marriage does not exist.

I have shared these few observations to give you a brief review of the *possible enemies* that may have destroyed your marriage. I am not suggesting that you blame everyone else, but that you avoid some of these mistakes *as you build a new future.*

If Divorce Happens

God is anti-divorce.

He is against *anything* that hurts and crushes people. Divorce is a heartache to God. "The Pharisees came...and asked Him [Jesus], Is it lawful for a man to put away his wife? tempting Him. And He answered...What did Moses command you? And they said, Moses suffered to write a bill of divorcement, and to put her away. And Jesus answered...For the hardness of your heart he wrote you this precept. What therefore God hath joined together, let not man put asunder" (Mark 10:2-5,9).

> *Wisdom Key #37*
>
> *God Never Consults Your Past To Determine Your Future.*

Some people *refuse* to put forth any effort to make a marriage work. You must *face* this fact.

Some marriage partners contemptuously cross the boundary lines of faithfulness and flaunt their so-called freedom as they crush the hearts of their mates through infidelity. Others willingly become slaves of alcoholism and drug addiction, leaving their mates to scrape, scrimp and exhaust their life energy to pay bills and provide for their children.

You cannot change the nature of another person.

Only God can. And only with that person's permission.

You cannot force someone to love you. Increasing your sensuality has never guaranteed a faithful mate. Faithfulness is a *condition of the heart,* not merely the surrounding circumstances.

So, let's move on into a New Future, as we cross this Bridge called Divorce.

Wisdom Key #38

Those Who Created Yesterday's Pain Do Not Control Tomorrow's Potential.

8 Milestones On The Bridge Of Divorce

My own experience of divorce affected me dramatically. I wept for days, weeks, months. My mind was in shambles. My heart was broken.

Rebuilding seemed impossible.

That is when God taught me a very important truth: Divorce is not a dead-end street. It is a bridge to a different future. Divorce connects you to another dimension of God's world.

1. *Your Heart.* Divorce creates broken hearts. Not only a husband or wife, but the children left behind.

Wrecked.

Tormented.

You feel betrayed.

Rejected.

Wisdom Key #39

Misery Is A Yesterday Person Trying To Get Along With A Tomorrow God.

Your individuality and uniqueness were not desired, respected, nor pursued. Your love was unreturned.

I am so thankful for a loving Heavenly Father Who promised to give us *new* hearts. "A new heart... and a new spirit will I put within you" (Ezekiel 36:26).

2. *Your Mind.* When you experience divorce, *memory can appear to be your enemy.* It replays the past pain.

God has to heal your memory.
Time will not.

Sadly, I have met people who have been divorced for 20 years who still spewed out bitterness, hurt and their pain.

▶ *Change Your Focus.*
▶ *Stop Looking Backward And Start Looking Forward.*

Isaiah 26:3 says, "Thou wilt keep him in perfect peace, whose mind is stayed on Thee: because he trusteth in Thee."

▶ *Your Conversation Must Change.* You must stop discussing your former mate. "Whatsoever things are true... honest...just... pure...lovely...of good report; if there be any virtue, and...praise, think on these things"

Wisdom Key #40
Your Measure Of Forgiveness To Another Determines God's Measure Of Forgiveness To You.

Wisdom Key #41
If Time Heals, God Is Unnecessary.

(Philippians 4:8).

▶ *Your Former Mate Is Not Your Enemy.*

▶ *Satan Is Your Adversary.*

▶ *Divorce Is The Result Of Your Battle With Satan.* Yes, it is a loss, a failure... but it does not have to be fatal, or final.

▶ *God Can Begin To Piece Your Life Together Again.*

Divorce will constantly be in your mind. Naturally, whatever you think about decides the direction of your life.

I remember when I would get so depressed that I could not think straight. I would be eating a meal in a restaurant and just break down and weep.

My mind was *disjointed.* My thoughts were *fragmented.* I could not remain focused on any goals or dreams very long. *In fact, I quit dreaming for several years.*

Most of your battles will be *inside your head.* That is why your thoughts must be focused on God's new future for you.

You must think *ahead...*not *behind.* "Remember ye not the former things, neither consider the things of old. Behold, I will do a new thing; now it shall spring forth; shall ye not know it? I will even make a way in the wilderness, and rivers in the desert" (Isaiah 43:18,19).

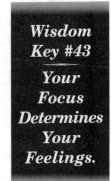

Wisdom Key #42

Stop Looking At What You Can See And Start Looking At What You Can Have.

Wisdom Key #43

Your Focus Determines Your Feelings.

3. *Your Social Acceptance.* Friends suddenly change...couples distance themselves from you. Your close friends may even become jealous that you might suddenly "prey" on their mates.

People in the church mutter between themselves, "There's two sides to everything...I wonder what we haven't found out yet."

Believe me, I felt some of the same distancing in my own life. Especially because I was a "minister". I was supposed to have all the answers!

People called friends of mine and lied about me. Some even believed part of these lies.

Slander is deadly.

That is when I learned it was not always my personal responsibility to *prove* my integrity, but the responsibility of others to *discern* it.

It was a magnificent day for my life when I permitted God to *reassemble new relationships* with those who chose to believe in me and *recognized* the presence of God within me. "When a man's ways please the Lord, He maketh even his enemies to be at peace with him" (Proverbs 16:7).

Most importantly, you must:

▶ *Avoid The Temptation To Justify Yourself.*
▶ *Suppress The Urge To Discredit Your Former Mate To Others.*
▶ *Keep A Peaceful Tongue.* You Will See The Benefits In the Future.
▶ *Take The Initiative To Attend Special*

> **Wisdom Key #44**
>
> *False Accusation Is The Last Stage Before Supernatural Promotion.*

Singles' Seminars And Services. Swallow your pride. While it is normal to withdraw, *do not let pride poison your future. Mingle.* Associate with others. Initiate *healthy* relationships.

4. *Your Sexual Needs.* Some religious teachings ignore this tremendous drive within mankind, *but it exists.* There is a need for *physical* affection.

Someone has said that even babies die when they fail to receive physical touching and caring. There is a desire to give yourself to someone. Someone to hold. Someone to hug. Someone to converse with.

Satan will use these moments... Seasons of Loneliness...to discourage you in your pursuit and maintenance of a holy life.

You see, you can be married and still be lonely. You can be in a crowd, and still feel lonely.

Loneliness is a *Spirit-need. Distinguish the difference.*

Satisfying the need for touching and physical affection can be alleviated in several ways: affection with your children...your parents and family...enjoyable fellowship with other members of the body of Christ at church. And most of all, focusing on spiritual matters in every conversation.

First Thessalonians 5:22 says, "Abstain from all appearance of evil." In a generation that promotes sensuality, the real cure for

> **Wisdom Key #45**
>
> *Loneliness Is Not The Absence Of Affection, But The Absence Of Direction.*

loneliness is to *stay submitted* to the Spirit of God.

5. *Your Relationships.* After divorce, you may feel differently toward the couples and friendships you have known in the past. You may feel like a "fifth wheel." Unwanted.

Or, you may even feel that they are showing you interest and caring out of pity. This is even worse!

You will be tempted to discuss all the details of your divorce with everyone you meet. It fills up your mind, your thoughts. You think everyone else is thinking about it also. They are not.

It is important that you confide *only* in a very select group of intercessors who are close to your heart.

You see, everyone who discusses your divorce with you is not trustworthy. You will be misinterpreted, misquoted, and ill-advised.

Your pain can be *productive.* God will send others during this season of your life for you to minister to and bless. Focus on *their* needs instead of your own.

Wisdom Key #46

Never Discuss Your Problem With Someone Incapable Of Solving It.

I learned this as I insisted to God that I was incapable of helping others, due to my own sense of loss, guilt and loneliness.

That is when He showed me the secret of Job. "The Lord turned the captivity of Job, *when he prayed for his friends:* also the Lord gave Job twice as much as...before" (Job 42:10).

▶ *Permit Others An Opportunity To Contribute To Your Healing.* Isolation

Is Deadly. One of the ways you can always discern when satan has intensified an attack on your life is when you have a desire to isolate from people. *Avoid withdrawal.* "Where no counsel is, the people fall: but in the multitude of counsellors there is safety" (Proverbs 11:14).

> **Wisdom Key #47**
>
> *When God Gets Ready To Bless You, He Brings A Person Into Your Life.*

▶ *Seek Out Qualified Prayer Partners.* "If two of you shall agree on earth as touching any thing...it shall be done for them of My Father" (Matthew 18:19).

▶ *Avoid Unwise Relationships During Your Seasons Of Vulnerability That Follow The Breakup Of Your Marriage.* Your life will become like a huge, empty space...a gap...a vacuum. Someone has left your life. *You will feel it.*

It is only natural to start trying to fill up that void with *another person, another project, another career.*

> **Wisdom Key #48**
>
> *Respect Those God Has Assigned And Qualified To Help You.*

▶ *Be Careful.* Satan often deals a *secondary* but crushing blow *to destroy your human hope.* He will introduce you to a *second wave* of failure through a *distracting relationship* that *detours* you and *diverts your attention away from God.* Satan's goal is to demolish any morsel of confidence in God that remains in your life.

What Can You Do?

▶ *Start Surrounding Yourself With Healthy, God-Conscious Friendships That Help You Prioritize Your Daily Life.* Again, I remind you of Proverbs 13:20, "He that walketh with wise men shall be wise: but a companion of fools shall be destroyed."

▶ *Utilize Your Extra Time To Rebuild Your Family Relationships.* A marriage breakup produces spare time. You must fill those empty hours with *productivity.* This is why I suggest reinforcement of your *family* relationships. "Have no fellowship with the unfruitful works of darkness, but rather reprove them" (Ephesians 5:11).

> *Wisdom Key #49*
>
> *The Worth Of Any Relationship Can Be Measured By Its Contribution To Your Priorities.*

▶ *Remember: Pain Is Transferable.* Do not exchange bitter conversation with others who like to help you reopen the wounds of the past. This simply *multiplies* your own hurt and *intensifies* your inner pain.

6. *Your Finances.* What men take away, God

will restore. In fact, I wrote a powerful song during this season of my life:

What Men Take Away, God Will Restore[3]

What men take away, God will restore!
When He gives back, He always gives more!
Never fear when you lose what you hold dear!
What men take away, God will restore!

Job is a study in *restoration. The Lord blessed the latter end of Job more than his beginning.* James even referred to him many years later in the New Testament. "Behold, we count them happy which endure. Ye have heard of the patience of Job, and have seen...that the Lord is...of tender mercy" (James 5:11).

Do not exhaust your energy trying to recapture your past. *Focus on the productivity of tomorrow.*

I experienced total loss and wipeout. My credit cards were stolen and high bills run up. My attorney's bills had to be paid including the attorneys who opposed me! My car was stolen and totaled out. I lost my furniture, my home...everything, with a single stroke of the judge's pen.

But I learned something.

I still had the Giver, even though I had lost the gifts. As long as you have the Source, recovery is guaranteed.

▶ *View The Financial Loss As A Season Of Learning And Rebuilding.* It is not easy. Perhaps your two-income family now has

---

[3]Used by permission. Win-Song Productions, Inc. Mike Murdock

one income. Attorney bills are high. Changes are dramatic. It sometimes takes years for people to financially recover from a divorce.

Wisdom Key #50

Crisis Is Merely A Season For Creativity.

But, you *can* recover.

I experienced continuous periods of depression following my financial losses. For almost a year, I lived in a small one-bedroom apartment with no furniture. For another year, I lived with friends in a tiny bedroom in their home on the West Coast.

But, I remembered the multimillionaires in history who experienced the same type of setbacks and bankruptcies and drew strength from their example.

▶ *Be Willing To Discipline Yourself For A Season.*

This is where I learned Seed-faith.

God began to teach me that I still possessed something. I had *faith.* I had the *knowledge of God.* I began to learn that *you always have enough in your hand to create something you do not have.* (Be sure to read the chapter on finances in this book.)

▶ *Be Willing To Cut Back On A Flamboyant Lifestyle.* It will not kill you!

▶ *Tighten The Budget.*

▶ *Consider A Second Job.* It will not even hurt you to get a part-time secondary job during this season of rebuilding.

▶ *Whatever You Do, Keep Sowing Your Tithes And Offerings Into God's Work.* Expect

Him to honor you where and when you need it the most.

7. *Your Faith In God.* You will be tempted to *doubt* God...His love for you...His power to change others' lives. There is nothing more infuriating or helpless than waiting to see a former mate *change...* without success.

> *Wisdom Key #51*
>
> *You Have No Right To Anything You Have Not Pursued.*

I am sure Joseph felt the same way when his brothers turned against him. But he discerned something very powerful. He knew that *what they meant for evil, God would turn for His good.* "All things work together for good to them that love God, to them who are called according to His purpose" (Romans 8:28).

Your mind will resent its inability to understand the divorce. But your faith can still work for you in God's next chapter of your life.

Remember divorce is a bridge. It is not a dead-end road. *It can take you somewhere. Exactly Where God Wants You To Be.*

▶ *Work To Rebuild Your Faith In God.*
▶ *Listen To Scriptures On Cassette Tapes.*
▶ *Listen To The Strong Faith Teachings Of Great Men Of God.*
▶ *Absorb The "Spirit Of Battle" That These Men Possess To Stand Against The Wiles And Efforts Of Satan's Attempt To Destroy Your Life.* (Be sure to read the chapter on spiritual warfare in this book.) You will

need the strength of someone with "punch"...*the ability to fight back against satanic opposition.* This will build your faith.

▶ *Carry "Faith Cards" With You.* (I wrote out special Scriptures on 3 x 5 cards that reminded me to focus on my *future,* instead of my past.)

▶ *Stay Teachable.*

▶ *Do Not Enter The Arena Of Debate.* Your closest friends may say unkind things. Some may not give you a fair opportunity to explain yourself or your circumstances. Some will be rigid and legalistic in their judgment of you.

▶ *God Will Vindicate You Through His Special Blessings.* "A wise man will hear, and will increase learning...a man of understanding shall attain unto wise counsels" (Proverbs 1:5).

> **Wisdom Key #52**
>
> **Faith Comes When You Hear God Talk.**

▶ *Be Discreet.* "Discretion shall preserve thee, understanding shall keep thee: To deliver thee from the way of the evil man" (Proverbs 2:11,12).

▶ *Refrain From Declaring All That You Know.* Your enemies will never believe you anyway, and your friends will not require a total explanation.

▶ *Honestly Confess To God Your Weaknesses,*

Failures, And Sins That Might Have Contributed To The Divorce. It is easy to blame everyone else for your personal failures. But it is equally important for you to face up to your personal responsibility.

Wisdom Key #53

Never Attempt To Teach A Non-Seeker.

▶ *Ask God What Changes Need To Be Made In Your Life.* God never prosecutes anyone who confesses. "He that covereth his sins shall not prosper: but whoso confesseth and forsaketh them shall have mercy" (Proverbs 28:13).

▶ *Allow God The Right To Judge Or Penalize Those Who Have Rebelled Against Him.*

▶ *Concentrate On Your Own Restoration And Recovery With God.*

8. *Your Ministry*

▶ *The Broken Become Masters At Mending.* You may seem fragmented today. Maybe you lack direction for your life.

You may be experiencing a lengthy *season of hopelessness,* a sense of futility, but *pain is like a factory.* Its products are compassion, caring and knowledge.

▶ *You Now Have Something To Give That You Have Never Had Before.*

▶ *Someone Else Around You Is Hurting Today.* They need you. They may hurt too much to reach. They may be too insensitive to discern that you possess their answer.

▶ *But Because Of Your Own Pain, Your Sensitivity Has Multiplied.* You are like radar. You are picking up their *signals of hurt.*

This is also *Miracle-time* for you.

▶ *It Is Your Opportunity To Multiply Your Own Harvest As You Sow Your Seeds Of Compassion And Caring Into Their Lives.* Concentrate On Their Recovery And God Will Concentrate On Yours. "Withhold not good from them to whom it is due, when it is in the power of thine hand to do it" (Proverbs 3:27).

> **Wisdom Key #54**
>
> *Forgiveness Is Permitting God The Exclusive Right To Penalize, Judge Or Correct Another.*

▶ *God Is Not Through Using You.* Even though there has been a chaotic period in your life, God still has plans. *His plans have not changed.* Satan has tried with all of his might to *abort* God's dream within you.

▶ *God Has Never Quit Dreaming Big For Your Life.*

▶ *God's Best Generals Carry The Wounds Of Many Battles.* You are not an exception. "The Longest Midnight Still Ends In Daybreak." God planned it that way.

▶ *Get Your Mind On Tomorrow.* Stop looking through the rearview mirror of life, and concentrate on the *road ahead.*

▶ *Do Not Exhaust Your Energy On Yesterday.* You were not created to carry the *pain of the past* and the *priorities of the future* simultaneously.

▶ *Release Yesterday.* Pour your energy into building tomorrow, not repairing yesterday.

> *Wisdom Key #55*
>
> *The Broken Become Masters At Mending.*

Divorce is a bridge, not a dead-end street. God is taking you to a *new* chapter, *new* friendships, *new* plans, *new* knowledge, *new* dreams.

Life is not over. You are birthing a magnificent season of greater ministry to others.

My Special Prayer For You

"Father, I know the pain of divorce. I know how this time of crisis feels. But I also know that You are still the *Healer.* Nothing is impossible for You.

In the Name of Jesus, forgive us our mistakes, our sins, our failures of the past. We release our former mates to You for total healing and correction.

Give us a *new* start...*new* dreams. We commit and surrender our lives to Your total correction and direction today. Thank You for being the *God of the Second Chance.* In Jesus' Name. Amen."

Receive God's Message Of Restoration

"When thou passest through the waters, I will be with thee...they shall not overflow thee: when thou walkest through the fire, thou shalt not be burned" (Isaiah 43:2).

"Remember ye not the former things, neither consider the things of old. Behold, I will do a new thing; now it shall spring forth; shall ye not know it? I will even make a way in the wilderness, and rivers in the desert" (Isaiah 43:18,19).

> ▶ *God Has A Plan For You.*
> ▶ *He Has A Way For You To Break Out Of This Crisis Called Divorce.*
> ▶ *It Is Time To Launch Forth Into The New Future God Has Created For You.*

Wisdom Key #56

Satan Always Attacks Those Who Are Next In Line For A Promotion.

Wisdom Key #57

Champions Are Rarely Chosen From The Ranks Of The Unscarred.

≈ 5 ≈

WISDOM KEYS FOR HANDLING CRISIS IN YOUR CAREER

Your Work Is A Photograph Of You.

Maybe you are out of work right now...and you have to find a job—*any* job. Or, maybe you have this horrible feeling that you are about to lose your job. You want to be prepared. Perhaps, you simply need a change. Or, you are just now entering the work force, and want to find the *right* job.

No matter what your circumstances are, God wants you to be *happy* on your job. Your work is designed to bring you fulfillment and joy.

Happiness is feeling good about yourself. It is based on your relationships and achievements. When your gifts and abilities are developed and utilized through your life's work, you grow in confidence and strength.

Unfortunately, however, most people waste their entire lifetimes working on the *wrong* jobs.

Are you one of these people?

Recently, I read some statistics that indicated seven out of ten people *despise* what they are doing, or the *company* for which they work, or the *career* that they have settled into.

This is tragic.

Most people live their lifetimes without ever discovering their own personal uniqueness, gifts and talents that God placed within them.*

They never discover their Assignment. Consequently, they never experience significant productivity. Therefore, they receive few promotions.

People seek an escape from misery at work through costly vacations, alcohol and drug abuse or some other destructive diversion.

I do not want you to fall into this category. This chapter contains *Keys* to help you *unlock* the Treasure of Accomplishment and Confidence in your work so you will be happy and feel fulfilled.

I want to help you overcome this time of crisis in your career.

Your Life's Work

▶ *Accept Work As God's Gift, Not Punishment.* First, you must realize that your

*Recommended Books: The Assignment (Volumes 1, 2, 3) Write: The Wisdom Center Box 99 • Denton, TX 76202

Wisdom Key #58

You Can Predict A Person's Future By His Awareness Of His Assignment.

Wisdom Key #59

Your Significance Is Not In Your Similarity To Another But Rather In Your Point Of Difference From Another.

work is important. In fact, it is a gift from God. "To rejoice in his labour; this is the gift of God" (Ecclesiastes 5:19). "The Lord shall make thee plenteous in goods... and...bless all the work of thine hand" (Deuteronomy 28:11,12).

> *Wisdom Key #60*
> *Your Provisions Are Wherever You Have Been Assigned.*

God has given your life's work to bring you personal fulfillment. It is a vital key to your self-esteem and significance.

If you are investing forty miserable hours each week on a job you do not like, two hours of church on Sunday morning will not necessarily cure it.

> ▶ *Recognize God As Your True Employer.* You must find *where* God wants you, *what* He wants you to be doing, and *move* as quickly as possible in that direction. Paul wrote, "With good will doing service, as to the Lord, and not to men" (Ephesians 6:7).

Discerning Your Career

> ▶ *Pursue Work Compatible With Your Abilities And Interest.*
> ▶ *Your Life Calling Is Usually Whatever Creates The Highest Level You.*
> ▶ *God Wants To Prosper You On Your Job.* Your work is

> *Wisdom Key #61*
> *Never Stay Where God Has Not Assigned You.*

one of God's most essential tools to bless you.
▶ *Work Is Ordained Of God.* Paul wrote, "If any would not work, neither should he eat" (2 Thessalonians 3:10).
▶ *Work Is A Tool For Achieving, Producing And Blessing Others.* Even in the Garden of Eden, God gave Adam and Eve instructions, "to dress it and to keep it" (Genesis 2:15).
▶ *Your Work Does Not Have To Be Easy To Be Enjoyable!* God wants you to be *happy!* Deuteronomy 12:7 says, "Ye shall rejoice in all that ye put your hand unto."
▶ *God Has Deposited Within You Seeds Of All The Gifts Necessary For Your Life's Work.*
▶ *You Must Discern Your Gifts And The Call God Has Placed Upon Your Life.* Then pursue work accordingly.

Throughout the Bible, men and women of God recognized and utilized their skills for the glory of God. Paul encouraged Timothy, "Neglect not the gift that is in thee" (1 Timothy 4:14). Solomon recognized skills (see 2 Chronicles 2:7).

Wisdom Key #62

What You Love Is A Clue To Something You Contain.

Wisdom Key #63

Go Where You Are Celebrated Instead Of Where You Are Tolerated.

Ephesians 4:11,12 discusses the gifts and callings God gave to His church: apostles, prophets, evangelists, pastors and teachers... "For the perfecting of the saints, for the work of the ministry, for the edifying of the body of Christ."

Analyze and review your present or most recent job, your gifts and talents, and discern what God wants you to be doing with your life.

> *Wisdom Key #64*
>
> *Your Assignment Will Require Seasons Of Preparation.*

▶ *Ask God For Wisdom About Your Career And Talents.* "If any of you lack Wisdom, let him ask of God, that giveth to all men liberally...and it shall be given him" (James 1:5). Be sure to seek God's Wisdom before you make any decisions.

Your 7 Question Job Analysis

1. *Are You Really Happy With What You Are Presently Doing?* Your personal excitement and enthusiasm about your productivity each day is so important. Nobody else can answer this but *You.*

2. *Is Your Present Job Actually A Short-range Or A Long-range Goal?* For instance, high school or college students may not intend to work their entire lifetimes

> *Wisdom Key #65*
>
> *Your Assignment May Require You To Walk Away From Something That Is Comfortable.*

at fast food restaurants. So their "after school" job is a *short-range goal.* They are gaining education, experience and basic financial provision.

Likewise, you should clarify in your own mind the *real* reasons why you have chosen to work where you are presently working or where you desire to work.

3. *Are Your God-Given Gifts And Strongest Talents Being Developed?* Prosperity and promotion usually come to those who totally focus on their most significant skills.

4. *Are You Working Just To Pay Your Bills And Have Fun Or To Truly Express A Contribution To Life And To This Work?* Prominent achievers go the *extra mile.*

5. *Do You Feel That God Is Satisfied With What You Are Doing Now?* I remember one tremendous guitarist who left a night club band after honestly answering this question. Though he loved his music, he felt God did not want him sowing his talents in such an environment.

6. *Do You Feel That You Are Doing The Highest Quality Of Work That You Are Capable Of Doing?* Millions cultivate the habit of mediocrity in their daily duties. If you are not striving for total excellence, you either have the wrong job or the wrong *attitude.*

7. *Do You Feel Like You Are Working "As Unto The Lord?"* You must see the work you do for your boss as work you are doing for *God.* If not, you will soon resent your boss and the time you spend on his work. This attitude will eventually cause you to feel unfulfilled and unproductive.

Seriously consider the above questions. Then,

ask the Lord for His instructions regarding your career.

How To Determine What You Really Want In A Job

1.   *How Much Income Do You Personally Feel That You Need To Consider Yourself Financially Successful?* Each of us have different needs. Some have 5 x 7 dreams. Others have 16 x 20 dreams. Neither is right or wrong. The key is to establish a true picture of your personal desires.

2.   *What Kind Of Problems Do You Really Love To Solve?* You can determine this by your favorite topic of conversation, favorite books and magazines that you enjoy. What would you *enjoy* talking about *the most? These things reveal your true interests.*

3.   *What Kind Of Environment Do You Find Most Enjoyable?* Some people discover that they need many people around them to be most productive. Others prefer solitude.

4.   *What Are Your Social Needs?* If your job deprives you of important relationships, it will become a source of discomfort and depression. You must diagnose the personal leisure and social needs that your happiness requires.

5.   *What Kind Of Family Life Or Time Do You Feel Is Necessary?* Obviously, a bachelor schedules his life differently from a family man with five children or a divorced mother of an infant. The job that is right for you should provide adequate time for sharing with those you love.

6. *What Level Of Social Approval And Respect Do You Need?* Each of us wants to be accepted by our friends. Never work for a company of which you are ashamed.

One man admitted to me that he had no confidence in the products he was promoting. Consequently, he experienced very little success. He left that job and went to work with a company he could honestly support. It made all the difference in his happiness.

7. *What Kind Of Financial Future Is Necessary For Your Peace Of Mind?* While very few jobs offer a lifetime guarantee, every one of us needs a sense of predictable income. *Tomorrow does come.*

4 Rewards Your Work Should Provide

1. *A Sense Of Worth, Pride And Significance.* Never speak lightly of your job if it produces a sense of worthiness or fulfillment, and is something that you truly believe in.

2. *A Sense Of Achievement And Progress.* You should feel that there is a real need for what you are doing, and that you are providing something worthwhile for other people.

Productivity is vital for happiness. Other people should benefit from something that you are doing every day.

3. *A Sense Of Personal Growth.* Your mind should be expanding, stretching and developing each day. Some people even change careers in the middle of their lives because of the monotony and boredom their routines produce.

4. *Sufficient Finances To Provide Adequately For Your Needs And Those You Love.* The Apostle Paul wrote, "But if any provide not for his own, and specially for those of his own house, he hath denied the faith, and is worse than an infidel" (1 Timothy 5:8).

It is vital that you honestly answer these questions before you can successfully release the four important forces that guarantee career success.

Set aside at least 30 minutes right now to write out detailed answers. The results may amaze you and set in motion a significant change in your future.

5 Reasons You May Be Unhappy With Your Present Job

1. Newly Discovered Disadvantages That You Had Previously Overlooked.

2. A Need For Variety Or Change That Your Present Job Does Not Provide.

3. A Lack Of Challenge In Your Present Position.

4. Unhappiness In Your Home Life That Is Causing Burnout Or Emotional Overload.

5. Personality Conflicts With Fellow Employees. You must recognize the reasons you are unhappy with your job. This will help you to prevent devastating mistakes in your future. Remember, your job is one of the most important parts of your life. One-third of your life is spent asleep. At least another one-third is spent on your job. It is really too important to ignore.

4 Forces That Guarantee Your Career Success

1.   The Force Of *Appearance:* "But the Lord said...man looketh on the outward appearance" (1 Samuel 16:7).

Most of us realize that we should not judge others by their appearances alone. However, the way you dress and groom yourself is a *message to others.* You are a "Walking Message System." It is just human nature to judge other people by the way they look.

The Bible has some fascinating observations. Proverbs 7:10 speaks of the "attire of a harlot." She dressed to communicate her desires and intentions.

Proverbs 31 speaks of the "virtuous woman" who was clothed in silk and purple.

Genesis 41:14 pictures Joseph as "he shaved himself, and changed his raiment [clothes], and came in unto Pharaoh." He changed his appearance *to create a climate of acceptance and influence* with the king.

The vice president of a major employment agency once said that the hiring of 90% of employees is mainly based on their physical appearance alone.

Recently, a young man had been complaining to his pastor that he could not find a job. The pastor shared the complaint with me and said that the congregation had been praying for the young man to get a job.

When I met the young man face-to-face, it was obvious why he had never been hired. His breath was atrocious. His hair was disheveled as if it had not seen a comb in two or three days. His shirt was opened revealing his stomach. The edges of his shirt cuffs were filthy. His shoes were unpolished and scuffed. While he lacked the finances to dress expensively, there was no excuse for his lack of cleanliness.

> *Wisdom Key #66*
> *People See What You Are Before They Hear What You Are.*

I am often stunned at the sloppiness of some people. *Your body is the temple of the Holy Ghost.* It is important to treat it with respect. Clothing covers 90% of your body, so *package yourself to create a climate of acceptance* with prospective employers.

2.   The Force Of *Aptitude:* "A man's gift maketh room for him, and bringeth him before great men" (Proverbs 18:16).

Find a job that is *compatible with the skills and gifts God has given you.* Unfortunately, however, most people never discover their greatest skills and gifts.

When Moses directed the building of the Ark of the Covenant, he hired people who were skilled. When Solomon directed the construction of the temple, he assigned jobs to people who were *specialists and experts* in their fields. "Every good...and...perfect gift is from above, and cometh down from the Father of lights" (James 1:17).

▶ *Attend Seminars.*
▶ *Increase Your Knowledge.*
▶ *Browse The Local Bookstore For Books Relating To Your Career.*
▶ *Subscribe To Magazines And Periodicals.*

▶ *Consult Others In Your Field Of Interest.*

Do not hesitate to secure a list of their favorite or most helpful books that they have read over the years.

Your salary usually depends on your responsibilities. When you increase your productivity, your salary will usually rise to that level of effectiveness.

> ▶ An estimated 84% of workers demand *constant supervision* to assure the completion of their tasks and work.
>
> ▶ Another 14% require *some* supervision.
>
> ▶ *Only 2% of the workers of America will work and complete their tasks and responsibilities without any supervision whatsoever.*

They are self-motivated.

They are achievers.

They are the highest paid. "Seest thou a man diligent in his business? He shall stand before kings" (Proverbs 22:29). "The hand of the diligent shall bear rule" (Proverbs 12:24).

3. The Force Of *Attitude:* "Servants, be obedient to them that are your masters according to the flesh, with fear and trembling, in singleness of your heart, as unto Christ; Not with eyeservice, as menpleasers; but as the servants of Christ, doing the will of God from the heart" (Ephesians 6:5,6).

> ▶ *Your Attitude Can Cause You To Rise To The Top Of*

Wisdom Key #67

Your Worth To Your Boss Is Determined By The Problems You Solve For Him.

Your Company Or Stay Where You Are.

▶ *Your Primary Attitude Should Be That Of A Servant:* "Whosoever will be chief among you, let him be your servant" (Matthew 20:27). This is the true spirit of Christ, that of a servant.

▶ *Learn To Respect Your Employer "In The Lord."* You see, God is in authority over your boss. You actually are working for God.

▶ *Use Criticism To Your Advantage.* In fact, get on the positive side of it: *Ask* your boss for suggestions and correction. "Poverty and shame shall be to him that refuseth instruction: but he that regardeth reproof shall be honoured" (Proverbs 13:18).

▶ *Give Praise And Encouragement When Appropriate.* "A word spoken in due season, how good is it!" (Proverbs 15:23).

▶ *Do Not Flatter Others To Get Ahead.* Avoid giving undeserved praise. "As he that bindeth a stone in a sling, so is he that giveth honour to a fool" (Proverbs 26:8). "A flattering mouth worketh ruin" (Proverbs 26:28). "He that rebuketh a man afterwards shall find more favour than he that flattereth with the

Wisdom Key #68

You Will Only Be Remembered For Two Things: The Problems You Solve Or The Ones You Create.

tongue" (Proverbs 28:23).

▶ *Do Not Become A Complainer Or A Murmurer On Your Job.* It is true that the squeaky wheel gets the grease, but as my brother, John, often says, *"It is also the first one that gets replaced!"*

The Israelites never tasted the grapes of Canaan *because of their attitude, not* because of the Giants of Adversity. "When the people complained, it displeased the Lord...and the fire of the Lord burnt among them, and consumed them" (Numbers 11:1).

> *Wisdom Key #69*
>
> *God Will Never Advance You Beyond Your Last Disobedience.*

▶ *Harness Anger And Control Your Spirit.* "He that hath no rule over his own spirit is like a city that is broken down, and without walls" (Proverbs 25:28). "He that is soon angry dealeth foolishly" (Proverbs 14:17). "He that is slow to anger is better than the mighty; and he that ruleth his spirit than he that taketh a city" (Proverbs 16:32).

▶ *Do Not Make Weak Excuses When You Resent Doing Something You Have Been Asked To Do.* "The slothful man saith, There is a lion in the way; a lion is in the streets" (Proverbs 26:13). Lazy people are always looking for reasons to get out of work. *Do not be one of them* if you want God to prosper you on your job.

▶ *Refuse The Bondage Of Bribery And The Influence Of Intimidation.* "A wicked man taketh a gift out of the bosom to pervert the ways of judgment" (Proverbs 17:23). "Be not afraid of their faces: for I am with thee to deliver thee, saith the Lord" (Jeremiah 1:8).

> **Wisdom Key #70**
>
> *Someone Is Always Observing You Who Is Capable Of Greatly Blessing You.*

▶ *Be Honest About Your Mistakes.* "He that covereth his sins shall not prosper: but whoso confesseth and forsaketh them shall have mercy" (Proverbs 28:13).

▶ *Do Not Be A Time-Thief.* Do not waste company time being unproductive. Be prompt in arriving at your place of work, and get busy quickly. "Let him that stole steal no more: but rather let him labour, working with his hands the thing which is good, that he may have to give to him that needeth" (Ephesians 4:28). "Redeeming the time, because the days are evil" (Ephesians 5:16).

▶ *Learn To Demonstrate Your Appreciation To Others Frequently And In Creative Ways.* Send telegrams. Flowers. Handwritten notes. Vocalize your compliments. Everyone around you treasures recognition of their worth. "In every thing give thanks: for this is the will of God" (1 Thessalonians 5:18).

▶ *Refuse To Gossip And Spread Rumors.* "Speak not evil one of another" (James 4:11). "He that covereth a transgression seeketh love; but he that repeateth a matter separateth very friends" (Proverbs 17:9). "A forward man soweth strife: and a whisperer separateth chief friends" (Proverbs 16:28). "The words of a talebearer are as wounds" (Proverbs 18:8).

▶ *Do Not Talk Too Much.* "Whoso keepeth his mouth and his tongue, keepeth his soul from troubles" (Proverbs 21:23).

▶ *Be Swift To Listen To And Complete Every Instruction From Your Boss.* "A wise man will hear, and will increase learning" (Proverbs 1:5).

Try to focus on your supervisor's long-range goals and what he is really attempting to do with the company.

▶ *Learn Everything Possible About Your Job.* "Give attendance to reading" (1 Timothy 4:13). "Study to shew thyself approved" (2 Timothy 2:15).

▶ *Be Quick To Ask For Help And Information When Needed.* "A man of knowledge increaseth strength...in multitude of counsellors there is safety" (Proverbs 24:5,6).

▶ *Be Warm, Friendly And Hospitable In The Spirit Of Christ.* Project Jesus in genuine

love and enthusiasm.
Resist the "holier-than-thou" attitude. "The servant of the Lord must not strive; but be gentle unto all men, apt to teach, patient" (2 Timothy 2:24).

> *Learn To Keep Confidences That Are Shared With You By Others.* Discretion is one of the most important assets that you can have. It is not something that you are born with, nor can purchase, nor go to college to receive.

> *Make A Decision To Bless The World Around You Through Your Attitude Of Love, Joy And Enthusiasm.*

4. The Force Of *Atmosphere:*

> *Everything You Do Creates A Climate.* Good or bad.

> *Everything You Say Creates A Climate.* Good or bad.

> *Your State Of Mind Determines Your Behavior.* Good or bad. "Whatsoever things are true...honest...just... pure...lovely...of good report; if there be any virtue, and...praise, think on these things" (Philippians 4:8).

> *You Are The Seed That Gives Birth To The Atmosphere Surrounding You.*

> *Your Atmosphere Repels Or Attracts Others.*

> *You Can Even Alter An Existing Bad*

Wisdom Key #71

Your Assignment Is To Solve An Existing Problem In Someone's Life.

*Atmosphere And Climate Through
Releasing Your Own Joy And Spiritual
Energy.* I call this being aggressively
happy.

Create an atmosphere of integrity, peace and stability, and people will enjoy being a part of your life.

Maintain an attitude of excellence and accomplishment, and God will see to it that you are honored and even promoted.

Paul instructed, "Study to be quiet, and to do your own business, and to work with your own hands, as we commanded you" (1 Thessalonians 4:11).

▶ *Refuse To Speak Your Fears.* "The fear of the wicked, it shall come upon him" (Proverbs 10:24).

▶ *Respond Positively To Any Task You Are Asked To Do.* "Whatsoever you do, do it heartily, as to the Lord, and not unto men" (Colossians 3:23).

▶ *Do More Than Is Expected Of You.* "Whosoever shall compel thee to go a mile, go with him twain" (Matthew 5:41).

▶ *Assist Others In Their Responsibilities When Possible.* "Withhold not good from them to whom it is due, when it is in the power of thine hand to do it" (Proverbs 3:27).

▶ *Ignore Any Slanderous Remarks About Others In Your Presence.* "Discover not a secret to another: lest he that heareth it put thee to shame, and thine infamy turn not away" (Proverbs 25:9,10).

▶ *Focus Your Mind And Total Attention On*

The Immediate Priority.
"The thoughts of the diligent tend only to plenteousness" (Proverbs 21:5).

▶ *Keep Accurate Records.* "Be thou diligent to know the state of thy flocks, and look well to thy herds" (Proverbs 27:23).

▶ *Discipline Your Work Or Desk Area To Generate A Business Environment, Not A Social Center At Company Expense.* "In all labour there is profit: but the talk of the lips tendeth only to penury" (Proverbs 14:23).

▶ *Target Your Enthusiasm, Smiles, And Love Toward Everyone, Even Those Who May Have Wronged You.* "When a man's ways please the Lord, He maketh even his enemies to be at peace with him" (Proverbs 16:7).

▶ *Communicate Clearly, Distinctly And Decisively Your Instructions To Those Around You So There Will Be No Possibility Of Being Misunderstood.* It is your responsibility to develop the ability to articulate and skillfully present your Assignment to those who are called of God to help you. "Death and life are in the power of the tongue...they that love it shall

> *Wisdom Key #72*
>
> *God Will Never Promote You Until You Become Overqualified For Your Present Assignment.*

eat the fruit thereof" (Proverbs 18:21).

▶ *Keep A Daily To-Do List And Establish Deadlines.* Know what you are to accomplish... "one thing I do" (Philippians 3:13). "To every thing there is a season" (Ecclesiastes 3:1). This creates an atmosphere of decisiveness and clarity.

▶ *Keep A Sense Of Movement And Progress At All Times In The Direction Of Your Next Task.* "Reaching forth unto those things which are before, I press toward the mark for the prize of the high calling of God in Christ Jesus" (Philippians 3:13,14).

Wisdom Key #73

Your Daily Agenda Should Be Built Around Your Assignment.

It was said that John F. Kennedy always kept a *sense of movement* in his presence. Those who discussed anything with him were treated graciously, but became conscious that he had something on schedule that he was *moving toward.* This eliminated time-wasters and trivial conversation. Strive to create similar currents around yourself.

▶ *Make Jesus Your Work Partner.* Keep God-conscious. "Thou wilt keep him in perfect peace, whose mind is stayed on Thee: because he trusteth in Thee" (Isaiah 26:3).

▶ *Never Stay Where God Has Not Assigned You.* Move as quickly as you possibly can in the direction of God's dreams and goals. You see, if you hate your work, you will eventually begin to hate your life. It will affect your marriage like a cancerous sore. It will destroy your relationship with your friends and your family. You must target your life *into the Will of God* and be where God wants you to be.

Do not forget...one-third of your life on earth is spent at your work. *You Alone Are Responsible For What You Decide To Do With It.*

My Special Prayer For You

Would you pray this brief prayer with me today?

"Father, I thank You for Your precious Wisdom Book, The Word of God. I ask You to *direct* my friend and partner today into the job or business that You desire. *Unlock* the secrets of our personal and unique gifts. *Multiply* this joy through promotions... recognition...and *honoring* the work of these hands according to Your Word. In Jesus' Name. Amen."

Now, make your decision that you *will* go on with God. You *will* trust Him to reveal your gifts and talents. You *will* believe that He will bless the work of your hands.

Begin today.

Crisis reveals. Crisis energizes. Crisis stimulates. Crisis makes you use your faith.

Crisis means you must change.

▶ *Change What You Are Doing.*
▶ *Change What You Are Saying.*
▶ *Change To Whom You Are Listening.*

▶ *Change What You Know.*

Allow God to start today bringing you through this time of crisis in your career.

❧ 6 ❧

WISDOM KEYS FOR WAGING SPIRITUAL WARFARE

Your crisis will end soon.

Keep your eyes on the vision God has given you. Your spirit is birthing your dream *now*. It will not be easy. It will take some growing on your part. It will require a struggle, but your dream *will* come if you continue forward.

You *will* make it through this crisis! Paul said, "We are troubled on every side, yet not distressed; we are perplexed, but not in despair; Persecuted, but not forsaken; cast down, but not destroyed" (2 Corinthians 4:8,9).

God is using this time of crisis to *educate* you:

▶ *About Himself*
▶ *About Your Assignment*
▶ *About Your Enemy*

"All the commandments which I command thee...shall ye observe to

> *Wisdom Key #74*
>
> *Whatever You Can Tolerate, You Cannot Change.*

> *Wisdom Key #75*
>
> *God's Purpose In Your Crisis Is Not Your Survival, But Your Education.*

do, that ye may live, and multiply...
and possess the land...Remember...
thy God led thee...in the wilderness,
to humble thee, and to prove thee,
to know what was in thine heart,
whether thou wouldest keep
His commandments, or no"
(Deuteronomy 8:1,2). "Blessed be
the Lord my strength, which
teacheth my hands to war, and my
fingers to fight" (Psalm 144:1).

> ▶ *Though Crisis And Battle Are Not Always Your Choice, Winning Is.* That is why your faith in God is so important.
> ▶ *God Anticipated Human Problems.*
> ▶ *This Is Why There Was A Cross.*
> ▶ *Though Your Failures Are Planned By Hell, Your Recovery Is Far More Organized By Heaven.*
> ▶ *God Has Prepared A Special Way Of Escape Out Of Your Crisis.* Trust Him To Reveal It To You.

Wisdom Key #76
You Will Never Outgrow Warfare, You Simply Must Learn To Fight.

"Though I walk in the midst of
trouble, Thou will revive me...The
Lord will perfect that which
concerneth me...When thou passest
through the waters, I will be with
thee...they shall not overflow thee:
when thou walkest through the fire,
thou shalt not be burned" (Isaiah
43:2).

"The steps of a good man are

Wisdom Key #77
Nothing Is Ever As Bad As It First Appears.

ordered by the Lord: and he delighteth in His way. Though he fall, he shall not be utterly cast down: for the Lord upholdeth him" (Psalm 37:23,24).

The Lord *will* hold you up and bring you out of this crisis...if you lean upon Him.

God has a beautiful future planned for you. Begin to look for it today. "If the Lord delight in us, then He will bring us into this land, and give it us; a land which floweth with milk and honey" (Numbers 14:8).

Battles are *any opposition, pain or difficulty* that you encounter while attempting to obey an instruction from God, or to *complete* His dreams in your life, or to *receive* a desired miracle He has planned.

In short, a battle is any pain produced during your efforts to satisfy God's expectations of you.

Pain is for a season. "Weeping may endure for a night, but joy cometh in the morning" (Psalm 30:5).

Daniel's desire to please the Lord in his prayer life brought him into a great battle. His obedience activated enemies that resulted in his Lions' Den Experience. But Daniel was victorious because he kept his faith in God.

Wisdom Key #78

All Men Fall... Great Men Get Back Up.

Wisdom Key #79

Losers Focus On War, But Champions Focus On The Spoils Of War.

Wisdom Key #80

Battle Is Simply Meeting Opposition On The Road To A Miracle.

Warfare surrounded the birth of Jesus. "For Herod will seek the young child to destroy Him" (Matthew 2:13).

Warfare will surround the birth of Your miracle.

> ▶ *Make Your Decision That You Will Not Lose. Dig Your Feet In.*
> ▶ *Stand Fast On The Word Of God...Until You Win!*

Wisdom Key #81

Pain Is Discomfort Created By Disorder.

"Submit yourselves therefore to God. Resist the devil, and he will flee from you" (James 4:7).

"Cast thy burden upon the Lord, and He shall sustain thee: He shall never suffer the righteous to be moved" (Psalm 55:22).

Who Is Your Real Enemy?

Before you enter battle, you must know who your true enemy is.

Believe it or not, your enemy is *not* just people! People are often *tools* of your true enemy. Paul wrote, "For we wrestle not against flesh and blood, but against principalities, against powers, against the rulers of the darkness... against spiritual wickedness in high places" (Ephesians 6:12).

Wisdom Key #82

Warfare Always Surrounds The Birth Of A Miracle.

> ▶ *Your Real Enemy Is The devil...satan...lucifer.* "Be sober, be vigilant; because

your adversary the devil, as a roaring lion, walketh about, seeking whom he may devour" (1 Peter 5:8).

▶ *He Is An Ex-Employee Of Heaven A Fallen Angel.* "I beheld Satan as lightning fall from heaven" (Luke 10:18). "The great dragon was cast out, that old serpent, called the Devil, and Satan, which deceiveth the whole world: he was cast out into the earth, and his angels were cast out with him" (Revelation 12:9).

▶ *Satan's Time Is Limited, So His Efforts Are Intensified.* "For the devil is come down unto you, having great wrath, because he knoweth that he hath but a short time" (Revelation 12:12).

▶ *Even His Power To Tempt You Is Limited.* "God is faithful, who will not suffer you to be tempted above that ye are able; but will...make a way to escape, that ye may be able to bear it" (1 Corinthians 10:13).

The Nature Of Your Enemy

▶ *Satan Despises God.* And

Wisdom Key #83

Pain Is Not Your Enemy But Merely The Proof That One Exists.

Wisdom Key #84

No One Has Been A Loser Longer Than Satan.

he hates anything that receives God's
affection.

▶ *Satan Is Quite Aware Of God's Unusual
Care And Protection Of You.* Satan reacts
with unbridled resentment toward us. His
reaction to the blessings upon Job is a
prime example (see Job 1:9-12).

▶ *Satan Is Deceptive.* Cunning.
Manipulating. The father of all lies.
Jesus said, speaking of the devil, "He was
a murderer from the beginning...there is
no truth in him...for he is a liar, and the
father of it" (John 8:44).

Why Does Satan Oppose You?

▶ *He Opposes You Because You Are A
Potential Source Of Pleasure To God.* "For
Thou hast created all things, and for Thy
pleasure they are and were created"
(Revelation 4:11).

▶ *His Real Enemy Is God.* But because he is
powerless against God, he attacks that
which is *closest* to the heart of God...you
and me.

▶*His Main Purpose Of Warfare Is To Pain
God's Heart, To Insult Him, To Frustrate
His Purposes In Your Life.*

▶ *He Wants You To Grieve God's Heart By
Doubting God's Integrity.* "God is not a
man, that He should lie; neither the *son* of
man, that He should repent: hath He said,
and shall He not do it? or hath He spoken,
and shall He not make it good?" (Numbers
23:19).

The devil wants to prevent the arrival of any miracle that would bring glory to God. Satan's aim is to:

> ▶ *Paralyze Your Planning*
> ▶ *Abort Your Dreams*
> ▶ *Destroy Your Hope*

> **Wisdom Key #85**
>
> *The Only Reason Men Fail Is Broken Focus.*

What Are Satan's Favorite Weapons?

1. *Delays*

Satan tries to thwart or abort the arrival of your desired miracles. He knows that a delay can weaken your desire to keep reaching. Daniel shares this kind of experience in Daniel 10:2-14, which we will discuss further later in this chapter.

2. *Deceit*

Satan is a master at deception and error. He knows that if he can infiltrate a generation through *erroneous* teaching, he can destroy millions. *One single falsehood* from the mouth of an articulate speaker can derail the dreams of millions.

> **Wisdom Key #86**
>
> *Satan's Favorite Entry Point Will Always Be Through Those Closest To You.*

Only eternity will reveal how many dreams have crashed on the Rocks of Prejudiced Teachings against divine healing, the Holy Spirit, or financial prosperity.

3. *Distractions*

Broken focus is the goal of all satanic attacks. "Turn not to the

right hand nor to the left" (Proverbs 4:27). Your
energy and time are too precious to waste on
unproductive friendships, unworthy criticisms, or
any other *distracting* interests.

4. *Disappointment*

With yourself or others. Refuse to replay the
guilt of previous mistakes, nor become preoccupied
with past losses, nor magnify the weaknesses of
others.

Maybe people around you think of you as a
failure...and maybe you even agree with them. But
the truth of the matter is *God created you to win!*

You are a Champion.

"Choose you this day whom ye will serve"
(Joshua 24:15). Are you going to give in to satan
and fail? Or will you trust God and win? The
decision is yours.

Be prepared for the enemy's attack. Know
where it is most likely to come from, someone you
love or trust. "For the son dishonoureth the father,
the daughter riseth up against her mother, the
daughter-in-law against her mother-in-law; a man's
enemies are the men of his own house" (Micah 7:6).

How To Predict Your 6 Seasons Of Satanic Attack

Wisdom Key #87

When Fatigue Walks In, Faith Walks Out.

1. *When You Become Physically Exhausted.*

I travel a lot. Sometimes, up to
20,000 miles in a single month. I
have noticed that my faith and
enthusiasm wane through fatigue.

In fact, satan's greatest attacks on your faith-life will probably happen when you get little or no sleep.

2. *When You Face A Major Decision Regarding Your Assignment.*

This may be in your career or even geographical relocation. Remember, you must patiently endure a crisis to receive the promotion. That is why patience is so beneficial. "The Lord is good unto them that wait for Him" (Lamentations 3:25).

Wisdom Key #88

Crisis Always Occurs On The Point Of Promotion.

3. *The Birth Of A Child Destined To Become A Spiritual Leader.*

It happened after the birth of Moses when Pharaoh commanded the male children to be murdered (see Exodus 1:16).

Also, the birth of Jesus as I mentioned earlier: "For Herod will seek the young child to destroy Him" (Matthew 2:13).

Great people of God often relate childhood adversities that threatened them in their early life.

Wisdom Key #89

All Great Men Attract Satanic Attention.

4. *When A Specific Miracle Has Just Left The Hand Of God Toward You.* Daniel waited 21 days for his prayer to be answered. When the angel of the Lord finally appeared, he explained the warfare that necessitated the assistance of Michael, the archangel, to help him (see Daniel 10:13).

Your battle is really a signal. It is announcing, "Something is *en route* to you from God today.

5.   *When You Make An Effort To Launch A New Ministry For God.* Jesus faced His wilderness experience just prior to His healing ministry (see Matthew 4). I have seen it happen, almost without fail. Each major project...new television effort...new church building program encounters extreme opposition or setbacks.

6.   *When You Are Next In Line For A Promotion From God.* When Joseph announced the dream that God had given him, his own brothers, in bitterness, sold him into slavery. His reputation of honor was stripped because of one lie from Potiphar's wife.

Each day of adversity in Joseph's life simply ushered him one day closer to the throne.

> *Wisdom Key #90*
>
> *Satan Always Attacks Those He Fears The Most.*

> *Wisdom Key #91*
>
> *Hell Only Reacts To Your Future, Not Your Past.*

Your 6 Most Effective Battle Weapons

You will never win a spiritual battle *through your own strength or wisdom.* "Not by might, nor by power, but by My Spirit, saith the Lord of hosts" (Zechariah 4:6).

"For the weapons of our warfare are not carnal,

but mighty through God to the pulling down of strong holds" (2 Corinthians 10:4).

"For though we walk in the flesh, we do not war after the flesh" (2 Corinthians 10:3).

1. *You Must Know And Speak The Word Of God.* "For the Word of God is quick, and powerful, and sharper than any two-edged sword, piercing even to the dividing asunder of soul and spirit...and is a discerner of the thoughts and intents of the heart" (Hebrews 4:12).

> *Wisdom Key #92*
>
> *You Will Never Win A Spiritual Battle Logically.*

2. *Your Conversations Should Reflect The Mentality Of A Conqueror.* "Death and life are in the power of the tongue...they that love it shall eat the fruit thereof" (Proverbs 18:21). The three men said before going into the furnace, "Our God...is able to deliver us from the...fiery furnace, and He will deliver us out of thine hand, O king" (Daniel 3:17).

> *Wisdom Key #93*
>
> *When You Say What God Says, You Will Start To Feel What God Feels.*

3. *You Must Take Your Authority Over Satan In The Name Of Jesus.* "The name of the Lord is a strong tower: the righteous runneth into it, and is safe" (Proverbs 18:10). "God also hath highly exalted Him, and given Him a name which is above every name: That at the name of Jesus every knee should bow" (Philippians 2:9,10).

4. *You Must Clothe Yourself In Spiritual Armor Each Morning In Prayer.* "Take unto you the whole armour of God, that ye may be able to withstand in the evil day, and having done all, to stand" (Ephesians 6:13).

5. *You Must Respect The Power Of Prayer And Fasting.* "The effectual fervent prayer of a righteous man availeth much" (James 5:16). "Is not this the fast that I have chosen? to loose the bands of wickedness, to undo the heavy burdens, and to let the oppressed go free..that ye break every yoke?" (Isaiah 58:6).

6. *You Must Pursue And Extract The Wisdom Of God From Mentors He Places In Your Life.* "A wise man will hear, and will increase learning; and a man of understanding shall attain unto wise counsels" (Proverbs 1:5). As one minister says, "Your mentor should be your greatest source of stress."

4 Forces That Shorten Your Season Of Struggle

1. *Your Speaking: Words of faith build you up in the Spirit.* Faith-talk is explosive (see Proverbs 18:21). *When God wanted the present to end and the future to begin, He spoke.*

Wisdom Key #94

Never Speak Words That Make Satan Think He Is Winning.

Wisdom Key #95

One Hour In The Presence Of God Will Reveal Any Flaw In Your Most Carefully Laid Plans.

2. *Your Singing:* Singing creates a climate satan cannot tolerate. Songs of worship and praise dispel demonic spirits as Saul discovered when David played the harp (see 1 Samuel 16:23).

Someone has well said, "Motion creates emotion."

3. *Your Sharing:* The prayer of agreement with others is extremely powerful. It is wise for you to initiate the prayer of assistance from intercessors. "Whatsoever ye shall bind on earth shall be bound in heaven...whatsoever ye shall loose on earth shall be loosed in heaven...if two of you...agree on earth as touching any thing...it shall be done for them of My Father" (Matthew 18:18,19).

4. *Your Seed-Sowing: Sowing creates partnership with God* that involves Him in your adversity. "Bring ye all the tithes into the storehouse, that there may be meat in Mine house, and prove Me now...saith the Lord of hosts, if I will not open...the windows of heaven, and pour you out a blessing, that there shall not be room enough to receive it. And I will rebuke the devourer for your sakes" (Malachi 3:10,11).

I have always observed significant changes in times of stress, battle and struggle when I have boldly unleashed the above Four Forces.

Never Forget 2 Battle Truths!

1. Your Battle Is Always For A *Reason.*
2. Your Battle Is Always For A *Season.*

Overcomers Are The Only Ones Rewarded In Eternity. "He that overcometh, the same shall be clothed in white raiment; and I will not blot out his name out of the book of life, but I will confess his name before My Father, and before His angels. Him that overcometh will I make a pillar in the temple of My God, and he shall go no more out: and I will write upon him the name of My God, and the name of the city of My God, which is new Jerusalem, which cometh down out of heaven from My God: and I will write upon him My new name. To him that overcometh will I grant to sit with Me in My throne, even as I also overcame, and am set down with My Father in His throne" (Revelation 3:5,12,21).

> ### Wisdom Key #96
>
> ### Battle Is Your Chance For Recognition ...Both In Heaven And Hell.

"Fight the good fight of faith, lay hold on eternal life, whereunto thou art also called, and hast professed a good profession before many witnesses" (1 Timothy 6:12).

Well, go ahead and get back up and going! Something good is en route from the Father to you today!

Special Memo To Spiritual Soldiers

▶ *Accurately Assess Your Struggle.*
▶ *Name Your Real Enemy For Who He Is.*
▶ *Make A Quality Decision To Go On With God.* You have already been in your past. There was nothing there that you wanted, so fight to get into your future.
▶ *Do Battle.*
▶ *Your Endurance Is Demoralizing To*

Satan.

▶ *The Rewards Of Overcoming Are*
  Worth A Thousand Times More Than Any
  Pain You Will Ever Experience.

The taste of victory lasts far longer than the memory of your struggle!

Please feel free to send any special prayer requests to my staff and me today. We believe in miracles and the Prayer of Agreement (Matthew 18:18,19). I will write you back a powerful letter of encouragement as soon as I hear from you.

MASTER KEYS FOR SUCCESS IN TIMES OF CHANGE

WISDOM KEYS

CHAPTER 1

WISDOM KEYS FOR TIMES OF FAILURE

1. Crisis Always Occurs At The Curve Of Change.

2. Success Is Satisfying Movement Toward Worthwhile Goals That God Has Scheduled For Your Life.

3. The Smallest Step In The Right Direction Always Creates Joy.

4. What You Are Willing To Walk Away From Determines What God Will Bring To You.

5. People Never Change What They Believe Until Their Belief System Cannot Produce Something They Want.

6. Failure Is Not An Event But An Opinion.

7. Failure Cannot Happen In Your Life Without Your Permission.

8. Failure Will Last Only As Long As You Permit It.

9. Any Act Of Obedience Shortens The Distance To Any Miracle You Are Pursuing.

10. God Always Rewards Reachers.

11. Faith Is Confidence In The Integrity Of God.

12. Satan Cannot Linger Where He Is Firmly Resisted.

13. What You Make Happen For Others, God Will Make Happen For You.

14. Your Words Are The Vehicles To Your Future.

15. Crisis Is Merely Concentrated Information.

CHAPTER 2

WISDOM KEYS FOR CRISIS IN YOUR LIFE PURPOSE

16. Your Purpose Is Not Your Decision But Your Discovery.

17. The Proof Of God's Presence Far Outweighs The Proof Of His Absence.

18. Prayer Is One Of The Proofs That You Truly Respect God.

19. God Never Forgets Anyone Who Makes Him Feel Good.

20. Obedience Is The Only Thing God Has Ever Required Of Man.

21. What You Love Is A Clue To Your Assignment And Purpose In Life.

22. People Who Feel Great About Themselves Produce Great Results.

23. He Multiplies Your Seed Back Into Your Life Where You Need It The Most.

24. Your Seed Is Anything God Has Given You To Sow Into Someone Else.

25. Your Reaction To Someone In Trouble Determines God's Reaction To You The Next Time You Are In Trouble.

Chapter 3

Wisdom Keys For Surviving Financial Crisis

26. Intolerance Of The Present Creates A Future.

27. Whatever God Has Already Given To You Will Create Anything Else He Has Promised You.

28. When You Let Go Of What Is In Your Hand, God Will Let Go Of What Is In His Hand.

29. Your Seed May Leave Your Hand, But It Will Never Leave Your Life. It Goes Into Your Future Where It Multiplies.

30. Your Seed Is The Only Influence You Have Over Your Future.

31. Your Seed Is A Monument Of Trust In The Mind Of God.

32. What You Believe Is Creating Your Present Circumstances.

33. Whatever You Have In Your Hand Is What God Will Use To Create Your Future.

34. When Your Seed Leaves Your Hand, Your Harvest Will Leave The Warehouse Of Heaven Toward You!

CHAPTER 4

WISDOM KEYS DURING THE CRISIS OF DIVORCE

35. Your Struggle Is Proof You Have Not Yet Been Conquered.

36. Satan Is The Source Of All The Pain You Will Experience During Your Lifetime.

37. God Never Consults Your Past To Determine Your Future.

38. Those Who Created Yesterday's Pain Do Not Control Tomorrow's Potential.

39. Misery Is A Yesterday Person Trying To Get Along With A Tomorrow God.

40. Your Measure Of Forgiveness To Another Determines God's Measure Of Forgiveness To You.

41. If Time Heals, God Is Unnecessary.

42. Stop Looking At What You Can See And Start Looking At What You Can Have.

43. Your Focus Determines Your Feelings.

44. False Accusation Is The Last Stage Before Supernatural Promotion.

45. Loneliness Is Not The *Absence* Of Affection, But The Absence Of *Direction*.

46. Never Discuss Your Problem With Someone Incapable Of Solving It.

47. When God Gets Ready To Bless You, He Brings A Person Into Your Life.

48. Respect Those God Has Assigned And Qualified To Help You.

49. The Worth Of Any Relationship Can Be Measured By Its Contribution To Your Priorities.

50. Crisis Is Merely A Season For Creativity.

51. You Have No Right To Anything You Have Not Pursued.

52. Faith Comes When You Hear God Talk.

53. Never Attempt To Teach A Non-Seeker.

54. Forgiveness Is Permitting God The Exclusive Right To Penalize, Judge Or Correct Another.

55. The Broken Become Masters At Mending.

56. Satan Always Attacks Those Who Are Next In Line For A Promotion.

57. Champions Are Rarely Chosen From The Ranks Of The Unscarred.

CHAPTER 5

WISDOM KEYS FOR HANDLING CRISIS IN YOUR CAREER

58. You Can Predict A Person's Future By His Awareness Of His Assignment.

59. Your Significance Is Not In Your Similarity To Another But Rather In Your Point Of Difference From Another.

60. Your Provisions Are Wherever You Have Been Assigned.

61. Never Stay Where God Has Not Assigned You.

62. What You Love Is A Clue To Something You Contain.

63. Go Where You Are Celebrated Instead Of Where You Are Tolerated.

64. Your Assignment Will Require Seasons Of Preparation.

65. Your Assignment May Require You To Walk Away From Something That Is Comfortable.

66. People See What You Are Before They Hear What You Are.

67. Your Worth To Your Boss Is Determined By The Problems You Solve For Him.

68. You Will Only Be Remembered For Two Things: The Problems You Solve Or The Ones You Create.

69. God Will Never Advance You Beyond Your Last Act Of Disobedience.

70. Someone Is Always Observing You Who Is Capable Of Greatly Blessing You.

71. Your Assignment Is To Solve An Existing Problem In Someone's Life.

72. God Will Never Promote You Until You Become Overqualified For Your Present Assignment.

73. Your Daily Agenda Should Be Built Around Your Assignment.

Chapter 6

Wisdom Keys For Waging Spiritual Warfare

74. Whatever You Can Tolerate, You Cannot Change.

75. God's Purpose In Your Crisis Is Not Your Survival, But Your Education.

76. You Will Never Outgrow Warfare, You Simply Must Learn To Fight.

77. Nothing Is Ever As Bad As It First Appears.

78. All Men Fall...Great Men Get Back Up.

79. Losers Focus On War, But Champions Focus On The Spoils Of War.

80. Battle Is Simply Meeting Opposition On The Road To A Miracle.

81. Pain Is Discomfort Created By Disorder.

82. Warfare Always Surrounds The Birth Of A Miracle.

83. Pain Is Not Your Enemy But Merely The Proof That One Exists.

84. No One Has Been A Loser Longer Than Satan.

85. The Only Reason Men Fail Is Broken Focus.

86. Satan's Favorite Entry Point Will Always Be Through Those Closest To You.

87. When Fatigue Walks In, Faith Walks Out.

88. Crisis Always Occurs On The Point Of Promotion.

89. All Great Men Attract Satanic Attention.

90. Satan Always Attacks Those He Fears The Most.

91. Hell Only Reacts To Your Future, Not Your Past.

92. You Will Never Win A Spiritual Battle Logically.

93. When You Say What God Says, You Will Start To Feel What God Feels.

94. Never Speak Words That Make Satan Think He Is Winning.

95. One Hour In The Presence Of God Will Reveal Any Flaw In Your Most Carefully Laid Plans.

96. Battle Is Your Chance For Recognition...Both In Heaven And Hell.

DECISION

Will You Accept Jesus As Your Personal Savior Today?

The Bible says, "That if thou shalt confess with thy mouth the Lord Jesus, and shalt believe in thine heart that God hath raised Him from the dead, thou shalt be saved" (Rom. 10:9).

Pray this prayer from your heart today!

"Dear Jesus, I believe that You died for me and rose again on the third day. I confess I am a sinner...I need Your love and forgiveness... Come into my heart. Forgive my sins. I receive your eternal life. Confirm Your love by giving me peace, joy and supernatural love for others. Amen."

DR. MIKE MURDOCK

is in tremendous demand as one of the most dynamic speakers in America today.

More than 14,000 audiences in 38 countries have attended his meetings and seminars. Hundreds of invitations come to him from churches, colleges and business corporations. He is a noted author of over 120 books, including the best sellers, *"The Leadership Secrets of Jesus"* and *"Secrets of the Richest Man Who Ever Lived."* Thousands view his weekly television program, *"Wisdom Keys with Mike Murdock."* Many attend his Saturday School of Wisdom Breakfasts that he hosts in major cities of America.

Clip and Mail

WISDOM 12 PAK

THE MASTER SECRET OF LIFE IS WISDOM
Ignorance Is The Only True Enemy Capable Of Destroying You (Hosea 4:6, Proverbs 11:14)

▸ 1.	MY PERSONAL DREAM BOOK	B143	$5.00
▸ 2.	THE COVENANT OF FIFTY EIGHT BLESSINGS	B47	$8.00
▸ 3.	WISDOM, GOD'S GOLDEN KEY TO SUCCESS	B71	$7.00
▸ 4.	SEEDS OF WISDOM ON THE HOLY SPIRIT	B116	$5.00
▸ 5.	SEEDS OF WISDOM ON THE SECRET PLACE	B115	$5.00
▸ 6.	SEEDS OF WISDOM ON THE WORD OF GOD	B117	$5.00
▸ 7.	SEEDS OF WISDOM ON YOUR ASSIGNMENT	B122	$5.00
▸ 8.	SEEDS OF WISDOM ON PROBLEM SOLVING	B118	$5.00
▸ 9.	101 WISDOM KEYS	B45	$7.00
▸ 10.	31 KEYS TO A NEW BEGINNING	B48	$7.00
▸ 11.	THE PROVERBS 31 WOMAN	B49	$7.00
▸ 12.	31 FACTS ABOUT WISDOM	B46	$7.00

Wisdom Is The Principal Thing

Book Pak
WBL-12 / **$30**
(A $73 Value!)

The Wisdom Center

ORDER TODAY!
www.thewisdomcenter.cc

1-888-WISDOM-1
(1-888-947-3661)

THE WISDOM CENTER • P.O. Box 99 • Denton, Texas 76202

Money Matters.

This Powerful Video will unleash the Financial Harvest of your lifetime!

▶ 8 Scriptural Reasons You Should Pursue Financial Prosperity

▶ The Secret Prayer Key You Need When Making A Financial Request To God

▶ The Weapon Of Expectation And The 5 Miracles It Unlocks

▶ How To Discern Those Who Qualify To Receive Your Financial Assistance

▶ How To Predict The Miracle Moment God Will Schedule Your Financial Breakthrough

Wisdom Is The Principal Thing

Video VI-17 / $30

Six Audio Tapes / $30 TS-71

Book / $12 B-82

The Wisdom Center

The Secret To 100 Times More.

In this Dynamic Video you will find answers to unleash Financial Flow into your life!

▶ Habits Of Uncommon Achievers

▶ The Greatest Success Law I Ever Discovered

▶ How To Discern Your Place Of Assignment, The Only Place Financial Provision Is Guaranteed

▶ 3 Secret Keys In Solving Problems For Others

▶ How To Become The Next Person To Receive A Raise On Your Job

Wisdom Is The Principal Thing

Video VI-16 / $30
Six Audio Tapes / $30 TS-104
Book / $10 B-104

The Wisdom Center

259

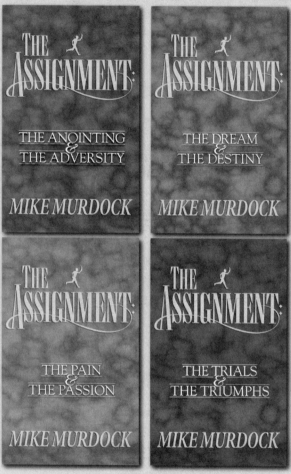

The Secret Place
Library Pack

Songs from the Secret Place

Over 40 Great Songs On 6 Music Tapes
Including "I'm In Love" / Love Songs From The Holy
Spirit Birthed In The Secret Place / Side A Is Dr.
Mike Murdock Singing / Side B Is Music Only For
Your Personal Prayer Time

Seeds Of Wisdom On The Secret Place

4 Secrets The Holy Spirit Reveals In The Secret Place /
The Necessary Ingredients In Creating Your Secret Place /
10 Miracles That Will Happen In The Secret Place

Wisdom Is The Principal Thing

Book/Tape Pak
SP PAK-001 /$30
Six Audio Tapes & Two Books
(A $40 Value!)

The Wisdom Center

Seeds Of Wisdom On The Holy Spirit

The Protocol For Entering The Presence Of The Holy Spirit /
The Greatest Day Of My Life And What Made It So /
Power Keys For Developing Your Personal Relationship With The Holy Spirit

Getting Past The Pain.

▶ 6 Essential Facts That Must Be Faced When Recovering From Divorce

▶ 4 Forces That Guarantee Career Success

▶ 3 Ways Crisis Can Help You

▶ 4 Reasons You Are Experiencing Opposition To Your Assignment

▶ How To Predict The 6 Seasons Of Attack On Your Life

▶ 4 Keys That Can Shorten Your Present Season Of Struggle

▶ 2 Important Facts You Must Know About Battle & Warfare

▶ 6 Weapons Satan Uses To Attack Marriages

Wisdom For Crisis Times will give you the answers to the struggle you are facing now, and any struggle you could ever face. Dr. Murdock presents practical steps to help you walk through your "Seasons of Fire."

▶ 96 Wisdom Keys from God's Word will direct you into the success that God intended for your life. This teaching will unlock the door to your personal happiness, peace of mind, fulfillment and success.

Wisdom Is The Principal Thing

Book B-40 / **$9**

Six Audio Tapes TS-69 / **$30**

The Wisdom Center

The SCHOOL of WISDOM

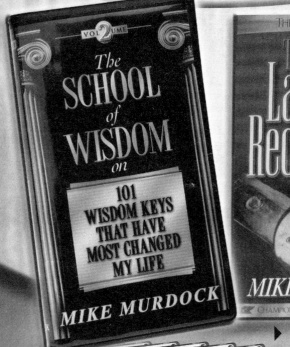

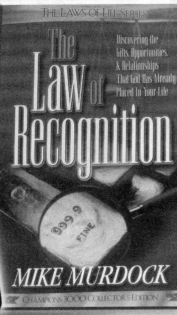

▶ 47 Keys In Recognizing The Mate God Has Approved For You

▶ 14 Facts You Should Know About Your Gifts and Talents

▶ 17 Important Facts You Should Remember About Your Weakness

▶ And Much, Much More...

▶ What Attracts Others Toward You

▶ The Secret Of Multiplying Your Financial Blessings

▶ What Stops The Flow Of Your Faith

▶ Why Some Fail And Others Succeed

▶ How To Discern Your Life Assignment

▶ How To Create Currents Of Favor With Others

▶ How To Defeat Loneliness

Wisdom Is The Principal Thing

Book/Tape Pak
PAK-002 / **$30**
Six Audio Tapes & Book
(A $40 Value!)
The Wisdom Center

Learn From The Greatest.

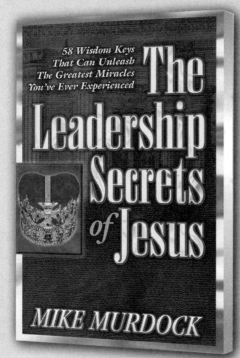

- The Secret Of Handling Rejection
- How To Deal With The Mistakes Of Others
- 5 Power Keys For Effective Delegation To Others
- The Key To Developing Great Faith
- The Greatest Qualities Of Champions
- The Secret Of The Wealthy
- Four Goal-Setting Techniques
- Ten Facts Jesus Taught About Money

In this dynamic and practical guidebook Mike Murdock points you directly to Jesus, the Ultimate Mentor. You'll take just a moment every day to reflect on His life and actions. And when you do, you'll discover all the key skills and traits that Jesus used... the powerful "leadership secrets" that build true, lasting achievement. Explore them. Study them. Put them to work in your own life and your success will be assured!

Wisdom Is The Principal Thing

Book B-91 / $10

The Wisdom Center

Your Rewards In Life Are Determined By The Problems You Solve.

▶ 3 Simple Ways To Increase Your Income In 90 Days

▶ 4 Keys To Recognizing The Problems You Were Created To Solve

▶ 12 Rewards Received When You Solve Problems For Others

▶ 5 Important Keys To Remember When You Face A Problem

▶ 2 Ways You Will Be Remembered

▶ 12 Keys to Becoming An Uncommon Problem Solver

▶ 6 Keys To Establishing Your Legacy

Wisdom Is The Principal Thing

Book B-118 / $5

The Wisdom Center

You can have it.

- ▶ Why Sickness Is Not The Will Of God
- ▶ How To Release The Powerful Forces That Guarantee Blessing
- ▶ The Incredible Role Of Your Memory And The Imagination
- ▶ The Hidden Power Of Imagination And How To Use It Properly
- ▶ The Difference Between The Love Of God And His Blessings
- ▶ 3 Steps In Increasing Your Faith
- ▶ 2 Rewards That Come When You Use Your Faith In God
- ▶ 7 Powerful Keys Concerning Your Faith

Dreams and desires begin as photographs within our hearts and minds things that we want to happen in our future. God plants these pictures as invisible Seeds within us. God begins every miracle in your life with a Seed-picture... the invisible idea that gives birth to a visible blessing. In this teaching, you will discover your desires and how to concentrate on watering and nurturing the growth of your Dream-Seeds until you attain your God-given goals.

Wisdom Is The Principal Thing

Book B-11 / $9

Six Audio Tapes TS-2 / $30

The Wisdom Center

Where You Are Determines What Grows In You.

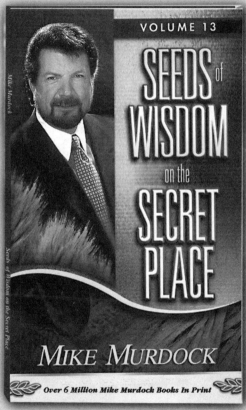

VOLUME 13

SEEDS of WISDOM on the SECRET PLACE

MIKE MURDOCK

Over 6 Million Mike Murdock Books In Print

▶ 4 Secrets The Holy Spirit Reveals In The Secret Place

▶ Master Keys in Cultivating An Effective Prayer Life

▶ The Necessary Ingredients In Creating Your Secret Place

▶ 10 Miracles That Will Happen In The Secret Place

Wisdom Is The Principal Thing

Book B-115 / $5

The Wisdom Center

Run To Win.

▶ 10 Ingredients For Success

▶ Ten Lies Many People Believe About Money

▶ 20 Keys For Winning At Work

▶ 20 Keys To A Better Marriage

▶ 3 Facts Every Parent Should Remember

▶ 5 Steps Out Of Depression

▶ The Greatest Wisdom Principle I Ever Learned

▶ 7 Keys To Answered Prayer

▶ God's Master Golden Key To Total Success

▶ The Key To Understanding Life

Everyone needs to feel they have achieved something with their life. When we stop producing, loneliness and laziness will choke all enthusiasm from our living. What would you like to be doing? What are you doing about it? Get started on a project in your life. Start building on your dreams. Resist those who would control and change your personal goals. Get going with this powerful teaching and reach your life goals!

Wisdom Is The Principal Thing

Book B-01 / $10

Six Audio Tapes TS-01 / $30

The Wisdom Center

THE SECRET.

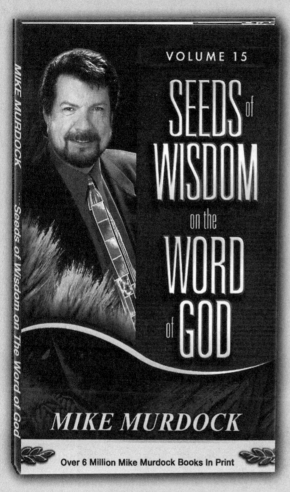

- ▶ 11 Reasons Why The Bible Is The Most Important Book On Earth
- ▶ 12 Problems The Word Of God Can Solve In Your Life
- ▶ 4 Of My Personal Bible Reading Secrets
- ▶ 4 Steps To Building A Spiritual Home
- ▶ 9 Wisdom Keys To Being Successful In Developing The Habit Of Reading The Word Of God

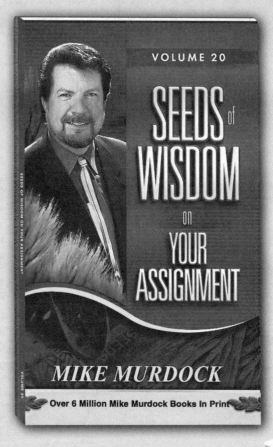

WISDOM COLLECTION
8

SECRETS OF THE UNCOMMON MILLIONAIRE

1. The Uncommon Millionaire Conference Vol. 1 (Six Cassettes)
2. The Uncommon Millionaire Conference Vol. 2 (Six Cassettes)
3. The Uncommon Millionaire Conference Vol. 3 (Six Cassettes)
4. The Uncommon Millionaire Conference Vol. 4 (Six Cassettes)
5. 31 Reasons People Do Not Receive Their Financial Harvest (256 Page Book)
6. Secrets of the Richest Man Who Ever Lived (178 Page Book)
7. 12 Seeds Of Wisdom Books On 12 Topics
8. The Gift Of Wisdom For Leaders Desk Calendar
9. Songs From The Secret Place (Music Cassette)
10. In Honor Of The Holy Spirit (Music Cassette)
11. 365 Memorization Scriptures On The Word Of God (Audio Cassette)